D1110147

Presented to:

_____

From:

_____

Meditations for Dog Lovers
Copyright © 2005 by Jim Dyet
Published by AMG Publishers/Living Ink Books
6815 Shallowford Rd.
Chattanooga, TN 37421

Unless otherwise indicated, all Scripture quotations are taken from The Holy Bible: New International Version®. NIV®. Copyright © 1973, 1978, 1984 by The International Bible Society. Used by permission of Zondervan Publishing House. All rights reserved.

ISBN 0-89957-394-0

First printing—September 2005

Cover designed by Meyers Design, Houston, Texas
Interior design and typesetting by Jennifer Ross, Chattanooga, Tennessee
Edited and Proofread by Jennifer Ball, Dan Penwell, Sharon Neal, and Warren Baker

Printed in Italy
11 10 09 08 07 06 05 –L– 8 7 6 5 4 3 2 1

*This book of devotions is dedicated to
everyone who is a dog's best friend.*

CONTENTS

1. Little Dog on the Prairie

MY WIFE, GLORIA, AND I had owned toy poodles; each had lived about thirteen years, but we had been dogless for eleven years. For the first five of those eleven years we lived in a town house and traveled frequently, so our circumstances didn't exactly scream, "Get a puppy." We probably got used to life without a dog during the next six years, but we were constant pet store window lookers and spectators at dog shows. I guess we both knew we were destined to own a dog again someday.

That someday arrived when we moved into a house and put up a backyard fence. I had accepted a new job that didn't require me to travel. It was definitely time to shop for "man's best friend"—one who would also be my wife's best friend, next to me, of course.

Gloria took the lead. She went online and took tests intended to help a prospective dog owner select the right pet: one whose temperament, size, and needs matched the inquirer's needs and interests. Some of the possibilities were Havanese, toy poodle, Chinese crested, Maltese, bichon frisé, Cairn terrier, and St. Charles spaniel.

At her prompting, I took some of the tests, too, with similar results.

Finally, one morning as I was scanning the newspaper's PETS classified section, I saw an ad for BEAUTIFUL, ADORABLE MALTESE PUPPIES. I called the phone number, and Gloria and I drove to the breeder's small ranch located thirty-five miles from our home in Colorado Springs. The Maltese paradise seemed out of place in the wide-open prairies where coyotes frequented and tumbleweed and rattlesnakes are common. But it was the birth home for our soon-to-be cherished and faithful family member.

Only one puppy remained unclaimed. Not much of a choice for serious dog shoppers. She had some fawn color on her ears and back—Maltese are supposed to be all white. But this tiny, silky puppy with a quiet demeanor and beautiful eyes stole our hearts. Because she was only four weeks old, we would have to wait about a month before we could take her home.

Anticipation and shopping for just the right kennel (crate), dish, collar and leash, the best dog food, toys, and treats filled our next four weeks. It was like preparing for the arrival of a new baby. We were soon to take responsibility for a little addition to the family, and our anticipation of the accompanying joy was running high.

GOOD DOGMA

I can't understand why my heavenly Father would accept me into his family. The Bible describes what I was when he set his love on me and bought me at an incredible cost—the blood of his Son, Jesus (1 Cor. 6:19, 20). Weak, helpless, and marred by sin, I must have looked totally unattractive to him. Nevertheless, he reached down, picked me up, and assured me of a bright future in his care.

Have you been brought into the heavenly Father's family?

A BIBLE TREAT

In love he predestined us to be adopted as his sons through Jesus Christ, in accordance with his pleasure and will.

(Eph. 1:5)

2. What's in a Name?

OUR FIRST FATHER, Adam, had a big job on his hands. According to Genesis, God brought the animals he created to Adam and tasked him with the job of naming them. I don't know what language Adam spoke, but I bet a number of names rolled across his mind when the world's first dog jumped into his lap. Arfie or Woofie might have been strong possibilities.

Our little dog on the prairie needed a name, and we wanted her to have one before we picked her up at the breeder's. "Little dog on the prairie" just wouldn't cut it. Can you imagine calling, "Here, Little Dog on the Prairie," or commanding, "Sit, Little Dog on the Prairie"? But choosing a name for her proved to be almost as difficult as selecting names for our children when they were born decades ago.

Knowing she was a Maltese, I favored the name Paula. You see, the Apostle Paul once shipwrecked off the island of Malta. Paula, a female form of the name Paul, would give her an almost biblical name. But Gloria nixed Paula because she associated that name with a politician she didn't like. A host of other names occurred to us, but for one reason or another we dropped them. A friend suggested Chocolate. When I asked why he would suggest Chocolate for a white dog, he explained, "She's a Malty. So why not Chocolate malty?!"

Finally, we settled on Molly—definitely a female name with a clear resemblance to the word *Maltese*.

Soon we were driving out to the wide-open prairie to claim our Molly and to bring her home.

GOOD DOGMA

When God accepted us into his family, he gave us names. For example, we're called children of God and sons of God. First John 3:1 declares, "How great is the love the Father has lavished on us, that we should be called children of God." Although the apostle John was about ninety when he wrote these words, he still reveled in the astonishing fact that he bore the name, "child of God."

The word translated "children" in 1 John 3:1 means "little born ones" and recognizes that we enter God's family when we are reborn spiritually (John 3:3–6). The term *sons of God* (Rom. 8:14 and Gal. 4:5) identifies us as God's mature sons and his rightful heirs. The two names, children of God and sons of God, speak volumes about God's love and about his goodness. He loves us as a parent loves a newborn baby, and he bestows upon us a rich inheritance because he sees us as his come-of-age sons and daughters.

Enjoy his love and appreciate every privilege he has bestowed upon you. Marvel at the wonder of it all!

A BIBLE TREAT

So you are no longer a slave, but a son; and since you are a son, God has made you also an heir.

(Gal. 4:7)

3. Bringing Molly Home

GLORIA, ALONG WITH OUR eight-year-old granddaughter, Jessica, and I were about as excited as three kids anticipating the arrival of an ice cream truck. Molly was now eight weeks old and ready to leave her mother and enter our family. The door to her kennel (crate) was open and so were our hearts. Puppy food, a doggy blanket, comb and brush, treats, water, and toys awaited her arrival.

Knowing that puppies have been known to throw up—or do something even worse—in cars, we put a cardboard box and paper towels in our Honda Accord before driving thirty-five miles east to claim Molly as our own.

She had grown since we had first seen her, but Molly was still a small ball of fluff weighing less than a pound. Gloria and Jessica took turns holding her while I took pictures. I didn't see any antelope in the background, but they must not have been far away. They thrive on Colorado's prairies.

Molly's first ride was uneventful. She curled up in Jessica's lap and, like a baby, exuded contentment all the way home. Also, like a baby, she later exhibited an animated side of her personality!

Once home, Molly got acquainted with her outdoor ladies' room and received a treat along with a "Good girl, Molly" for using it.

Soon she was settling in and exploring her new environment. Slowly, but surely, she would learn what was hers and what was not. A comfortable kennel was hers, so were a plush doggy bed, chewy toys, a doggy dish, a ball, and some squeeze toys. Our shoes were not hers. Neither were our toes!

Apparently, Molly liked her new home right from the start. Even that first night, she slept from bedtime until we woke her the next morning. We were going to get along just fine.

❖ ❖ ❖

Good Dogma

Before returning to heaven, Jesus told his disciples he would prepare a place in heaven for them and would one day return and escort them to their celestial home. That promise is valid for us twenty-first-century believers, too. We do not know when Jesus will return, but we know his arrival is imminent—it could take place any time. And when it happens, we will enter our heavenly home.

Everything about our home in heaven will delight us. Its brilliance will outshine earth's most radiant diamonds. Its beauty will be beyond compare. Its comforts will be perfect. And its furnishings will dazzle our senses. After all, the Carpenter of Nazareth is both the architect and builder, and whatever he does, he does exceedingly well.

Let's hope Jesus comes soon to take us home!

A Bible Treat

And if I go and prepare a place for you, I will come back and
take you to be with me that you also may be where I am.
(John 14:3)

Meditations for Dog Lovers

4. Purchased for Life

I NEED TO BACK UP for a moment and explain that it cost something to become Molly's owners. You probably know that buying a purebred, registered dog doesn't come cheap, but Gloria and I have never regretted putting out a few hundred dollars cash for our little dog from the prairie.

In the 1960s, we owned a toy poodle and bred her twice, once when we lived in Pennsylvania and later when we lived in Indiana. Each time, we offered the puppies for sale for $75. The transactions went smoothly in Pennsylvania, but one deal in Indiana went awry.

A young woman carrying a baby showed up at our Indiana doorstep and raved about the cute little poodle she wanted to buy. She dug into her purse and pulled out her checkbook.

I held the baby while she wrote a check. After a few minutes of pleasantries, she left holding baby and puppy in her arms. I offered to carry one or the other to her car, but she declined my offer. "My car is parked around the corner. I can manage okay," she said.

A few days later, I received notification from the bank that the check had bounced. I soon learned this woman had written bad checks all over town for everything from groceries to gas. Then someone from the police department called, saying she was in jail for writing bad checks. "She has confessed," the voice told me, "and she said you can go to her mobile home and pick up your dog. The door is open."

Not willing to enter anybody's home unattended, I asked a police officer to accompany me. He did and soon our poodle pup was home again.

This situation helped me to understand why the breeder on the prairie asked for cash when she sold Molly to us. Cash doesn't bounce!

GOOD DOGMA

Jesus bought us at the incalculable cost of his blood. Paul shared this fact with the Corinthians. "You are not your own," he told them. "You were bought at a price" (1 Cor. 6:19, 20). Peter, too, wrote about this purchase. He explained that we were redeemed (purchased) "with the precious blood of Christ" (1 Pet. 1:19). Although we cannot comprehend why Jesus died for us, we must admit we belong to him for the rest of our lives.

Knowing that Jesus paid such a price for us may boggle our minds, but it also delights our hearts. We take deep pleasure in contemplating his great love for us, and we gladly sing: "Now I belong to Jesus."

Belonging to him is far from enslaving; it is liberating and comforting.

A BIBLE TREAT

But you are a chosen people . . . a people belonging to God, that you may declare the praises of him who called you out of darkness into his wonderful light.

(1 Pet. 2:9)

5. Born to Please

GLORIA HAD LEARNED from an Internet search of Maltese dogs that they like to please their owners. That suits us just fine. Many years ago we purchased Bonnie, a shepherd mix that had other ideas. Whenever we opened our front door, Bonnie bolted and joined a pack. I spent more than a few days in my car patrolling the neighborhood to find her canine gang, apprehend her, and transport her back home—what she obviously considered a detention center.

Unfortunately, she never reformed!

But Molly was different. I knew she would never run away and join a pack of socially irresponsible dogs—even if they offered her a lifetime supply of liver treats. She deserved to wear a "Born to Please" tee shirt. She stayed close by and never showed any desire to stray farther than a few feet from us. Also, she seemed to want to listen to whatever we said to her. When we spoke, she cast her big puppy eyes on us and cocked her tiny head from side to side as if to catch every word and hang on to it.

A true lap dog, Molly loved for us to pick her up and place her into our laps. Of course, I claim she prefers to sit in my lap because whenever Molly curls up on my lap, she quickly falls asleep. My Lazy Boy recliner must seem like doggy heaven to Molly.

Good Dogma

Each of us—like Bonnie, the dog my wife and I owned a long time ago—has a history of bolting from God to run with the pack. We followed an aimless and reckless path that led us far from God. The prophet Isaiah charged that we had turned to our own way (Isa. 53:6). The apostle Paul described our lawless course as one laid out by the evil world system, the devil, and our sinful nature.

However, our lives are far different now. A dramatic change occurred when Jesus claimed us, and we yielded to his loving control. We experienced what the Bible calls a new birth. From that moment, we have wanted to please Jesus, our Master. We have been born to please!

A Bible Treat

We have not stopped praying for you and asking God to fill you with the knowledge of his will through all spiritual wisdom and understanding. And we pray this in order that you may live a life worthy of the Lord and may please him in every way.

(Col. 1:9, 10)

6. "Here, Molly!"

I WON'T FORGET the first time I set Molly on the floor, stepped several feet away from her and commanded, "Molly, come!"

How can she come to me? I wondered, knowing she was just eight weeks old and her legs were only about an inch long. Getting to me would surely take at least thirty minutes. Would she have the will and stamina to make the long journey? And why should she pay any heed to what I commanded? After all, I was still a stranger to her.

As if frozen in time, Molly stood motionless. Then she lifted her head and stared at me. Was she asking herself, "Who is this guy? Why should I obey him? If I go to him, will he be nice to me?"

But then a magic moment happened. One foot kicked out, then another and another and another. Molly came directly to me, and her tiny puppy gait spanned the distance in just a few seconds.

"Good girl, Molly," I told her gleefully as I picked her up and stroked behind her ears. She had obeyed my call, and I couldn't have been happier.

GOOD DOGMA

According to John 10:3, Jesus knows each of his followers by name. Whether you are Bill, Frieda, Gertrude, George, Henry, Juan, Ralph, Justin, Marcus, or Christine, he knows you personally. And just as Molly learned to respond when I called her name, so you and I are learning to respond to Jesus' call.

Sometimes he commands us to do tasks as simple as pray, read the Bible, and worship. But we may not respond very well at first. Gradually, though, we discover that the more promptly we respond, the better life becomes and the better we please our Master. Other commands demand a higher level of obedience.

A Bible Treat

The LORD came and stood there, calling as at other times, "Samuel! Samuel!"
Then Samuel said, "Speak, for your servant is listening."

(1 Sam. 3:10)

7. Molly Meets Dr. Lou

GETTING SHOTS IS NO FUN. I have had more than my fair share—the usual childhood shots, shots for college admission, shots for admission into the United States, pre-op shots, flu shots, and other shots I have successfully pushed out of my memory some time ago. Frankly, I would not feel slighted in the least if I never received another shot, and I am elated to anticipate a shot-free heaven. You can understand, then, how strongly I empathized with Molly the first time I took her to the veterinarian for shots.

After filling out a few forms at Dr. Lou's Sunnyside Veterinary Clinic, I placed Molly on the weight scales so the attendant could record her weight. Twenty ounces of fluff didn't break the scale, that's for sure.

Next, Molly and I went into a small room where Dr. Lou administered a round of shots while I held Molly and stroked behind her ears. Molly shook and whimpered a bit, but Dr. Lou's treats and verbal assurances calmed her down some. I reassured her everything was going to be okay. Little did she know she would later return for more shots and spaying. Nor did she know what I knew—all the hurting was for her good.

Although Dr. Lou and her staff were outstanding, I'm sure Molly filed the clinic in her memory bank under "Places to Avoid."

GOOD DOGMA

About a month after becoming a Christian, I learned that faith and trouble are not mutually exclusive. I had plowed my dad's '46 Hudson into the back of a pickup, and my only defense was, "Dad, I hit a patch of ice and couldn't stop the skid."

Dad didn't buy the excuse.

Decades later I can now look back on numerous trials and recognize that they actually bolstered my faith. Like Molly's shots, they hurt but were beneficial. According to Romans 5:3 and 4, "suffering produces perseverance; perseverance, character, and character, hope." Trials taught me something about my vulnerability and a whole lot about the need to depend on the Lord. I believe I emerged from each trial stronger in faith.

How often would you and I pray if everything went smoothly all the time? How motivated would we be to search the Bible for God's comforting promises? How hopeful of heaven would we be? How much like Christ would we be?

We may scream, "OUCH!" when trials strike us, but the divine grace accompanying each episode leads ultimately to a grand "HALLELUJAH!"

A BIBLE TREAT

In this you greatly rejoice, though now for a little while you may have had to suffer grief in all kinds of trials. These have come so that your faith—of greater worth than gold, which perishes even though refined by fire—may be proved genuine and may result in praise, glory and honor when Jesus Christ is revealed.

(1 Pet. 1:6, 7)

8. Microchip Molly

WHEN MOLLY TURNED three months old, she visited Dr. Lou for two services—spaying and to have a microchip implanted. Both procedures provided protection for her. Spayed, she would not get pregnant. Microchipped, she would not lose her identity.

Dr. Lou kept Molly overnight.

Upon arriving home, Molly wasn't quite as energetic as usual; but on a scale of one to ten, she registered nine. The spaying had hardly put a dent in her high-powered puppy booster rocket. She zoomed around the yard like a mini-white tornado and played at our feet exuberantly. Obviously, the prospect of never having puppies to honor her on Mother's Day did not dampen her spirits.

The microchip lay just below her skin, behind her right shoulder. The literature explained how authorities could scan the chip, checking it against national records to show her identification and ownership. The likelihood of someone returning her to us after becoming lost increased dramatically because of the microchip. That prospect made the cost of the implant a tremendous bargain.

Losing a dog can be traumatic, and unfortunately it is a common occurrence. You've seen those "Lost Dog" posters on community mailboxes, trees, and street signs haven't you?

LOST DOG: BLACK LAB, 2 YEARS OLD, ANSWERS TO THE NAME OF MISSY. LAST SEEN NEAR 5TH AND MAIN. IF FOUND, PLEASE CALL 555-5555. REWARD.

One day, while I was working in my church office and a women's luncheon was under way downstairs, a couple of frantic women hurried into my office.

"Help! There's a dog in the fellowship hall."

A Yorkie had entered the church and had made his way to the luncheon. I judged his weight at five pounds and his personality as amicable. Apparently, he simply wanted to make new friends. And who can suggest a better place than church?

A phone number on the dog's tag led me to the owner. Grandma answered the phone, but was unable to drive to the church, and her daughter and grandchildren were out searching for their lost pet. So I put the Yorkie in my car and drove to the address Grandma supplied. When I got there, the whole family was standing out front, eagerly anticipating the homecoming.

There's nothing like a lost dog to ruin a good day; and there's nothing like a recovered dog to turn the day into a big celebration.

GOOD DOGMA

I wish I could say I never strayed from my heavenly Father, but sometimes I cross the boundaries established in his Word. However, his love is boundless; he pursues me until he enfolds me again in his arms. Another benefit of belonging to my heavenly Father is I never lose my identity when I stray. I am still his child.

He sealed me with the Holy Spirit at the time of my salvation (Eph. 1:13). This sealing marks all believers as God's cherished possession. Our divine owner looks upon earth's population of billions of human beings and knows who belongs to him.

Of course the best and safest place for you and me is the center of our heavenly Father's will. Let's value that special place today and always!

A BIBLE TREAT

Now it is God who makes both us and you stand firm in Christ. He anointed us, set his seal of ownership on us, and put his Spirit in our hearts as a deposit, guaranteeing what is to come.

(2 Cor. 1:21, 22)

9. *It's Good for the Heart*

THE FIRST DAY OF every month Molly gets a chewable heart pill, crushed and mixed into her morning food. It must taste okay, because she doesn't push her bowl away or register a growl of displeasure. Any day would work for this once-a-month medication, but the first day is easy to remember.

The heart-pill description reads: "Each chewable contains 68 mcg ivermectin and 57 mg pyrantel as pamoate salt." The purpose of the medication is to prevent heartworm disease and to treat and control ascarid and hookworm infections in dogs. Now, that's impressive, but too technical for Molly and me. You would have to be a veterinarian or pharmacologist to understand the ingredients and how they work. But you don't have to be either one to reap the heart pill's benefits.

So Molly consumes her heart pill every month and stays healthy.

GOOD DOGMA

A theologian might describe the Bible as *theopneustos* (God-breathed). Further, he might claim that the only valid authority for our faith and life is *Sola Scriptura*. Given further opportunity to describe the Bible, he might use such words as inerrant, verbal and plenary inspiration, infallible, original autograph, and canonical. Whew! Isn't it a relief we don't have to understand those technical words in order to benefit from our reading of the Bible?

Just as Molly takes a heart pill once a month to maintain a healthy heart, so you and I can partake of the Bible on a regular basis to maintain robust spiritual health. But reading the Bible once a month won't accomplish the task. We need to read it every day, letting its truth penetrate our understanding and equip us for life in the real world. The following excerpts from the book of Psalms show us how to relate to the Bible and reap its benefits:

> But his delight is in the law of the LORD, and on his law he meditates day and night, he is like a tree planted by streams of water, which yields its fruit in season and whose leaf does not wither. Whatever he does prospers (Ps. 1:2, 3).

> The precepts of the LORD are right, giving joy to the heart. The commands of the LORD are radiant, giving light to the eyes (Ps. 19:8).

> I have hidden your word in my heart that I might not sin against you. . . . Give me understanding, and I will keep your law and obey it with all my heart. . . . Your statutes are my heritage forever; they are the joy of my heart. My heart is set on keeping your decrees to the very end (Ps. 119:11, 34, 111, 112).

Theologians might use some high-sounding, technical words to laud the Bible's character and extol the benefits of reading it, but for most of us it's good enough to say, "Get into the Bible every day, and let it get into you. It's good for the heart."

A BIBLE TREAT

All Scripture is God-breathed and is useful for teaching, rebuking, correcting and training in righteousness, so that the man of God may be thoroughly equipped for every good work.

(2 Tim. 3:16)

10. *Obedience School #1*

"I'VE KNOWN MALTESE OWNERS who had to get rid of their dog after only a few months. Some Maltese dogs have been in three or four different homes before they were a year old."

Gloria and I listened carefully to the dog trainer, while tiny Molly curled up in my lap.

"Molly likes to bite fingers. If you don't control that behavior now, she will bite when she is older, and you will have a big problem. Maltese are stubborn, so you need to establish your dominance as pack leaders."

Wow, I mused, here is three-pound Molly in a class with a huge Lab and an uncontrollable golden retriever, but the trainer is singling her out as the emerging canine criminal. What does this trainer have against little dogs?

In an effort to establish dominance, I followed the trainer's instructions to hold Molly prisoner in my arms, not allowing her to struggle for her personal freedom.

Next came the rollover test. Again, following instructions, I put Molly on her back and pinned her down. She proved instantly she was not a rollover kind of dog. Her feet flew frantically; her head bobbed rapidly; and she whined loudly.

"Sit," "Down," and "Stay" commands were standard parts of the obedience training, the 101 courses of doggy school.

As time progressed, Molly passed all the tests except the rollover test. She even learned to wait at a doorway until I walked through ahead of her.

Just one problem remained after Molly's graduation—she needed to obey Gloria, too. That would require more schooling!

Good Dogma

If you haven't read Psalm 23 lately, maybe you should read it again. It pertains so clearly to life. A caring dog owner provides for Bo or Brutus or Belle or Muffy or Max or Molly and teaches his canine friend to sit, stay, and follow. To a far greater extent, the Lord provides for you and me and teaches us to sit at his feet, stay by his side, and follow his leading.

We do not lack anything because Jesus is our Shepherd (v. 1). He prepares a table for us and fills our cup to overflowing (v. 5). He makes us lie down in green pastures (v. 2a). We follow him along peaceful waters and walk in paths of righteousness (vv. 2b, 3). Even when days turn dark and thunder bursts overhead, we don't have to fret or fear; he is with us (v. 4). And the best is yet to be—we are going to live with him forever (v. 6).

If you provide well for your dog, allow him to enjoy your presence, and lead and protect him—a dog's life can be pretty good. But the best life of all belongs to the believer who follows and obeys the Lord.

A Bible Treat

The watchman opens the gate for him, and the sheep listen to his voice. he calls his own sheep by name and leads them out. When he has brought out all his own, he goes on ahead of them, and his sheep follow him because they know his voice.

(John 10:3, 4)

A FEW WEEKS AFTER GRADUATING from obedience school, Molly enrolled in grad school or, more truthfully, another obedience school. The location was different. This time it was PetSmart™, and the students were different. Whereas Molly's classmates in the first school were big dogs, this time her classmates came in a variety of breeds and sizes. She could hang out with terriers and poodles if she wanted. Also, Molly would have a new teacher.

Something else was different. I stayed home. Now Molly could bond with Gloria. She would learn to sit, stay, and come to Gloria.

Obedience school #2 worked out quite well. The teacher seemed to understand dogs. He knew how to gain their confidence and friendship. More importantly, he knew how to encourage and educate the owners in the training process. After each session, Gloria sang the praises of Steve, the trainer, and Molly showed me what she had learned in class.

I don't know if PetSmart™ sang Steve's praises, but it should have. Thanks to him, the store sold beaucoup buckets of freeze-dried 100 percent pure beef liver treats. He used the treats as rewards for good dog behavior in class and recommended them to the students' "parents."

After class, owners followed by their dogs on leashes traipsed to the Dog Treats aisle and cleaned out the beef-liver-treats shelf. Then they lined up at the checkout to pay for the treats that would mold any dog's behavior into a thing of beauty and joy forever.

It was a happy day when Steve presented Gloria with Molly's diploma. However, it was not a happy day when the doorbell rang at home and Molly went ballistic, charging the front door like a lion charging an antelope.

Clearly, Molly needed more training. Was obedience school #3 in her future? It was, indeed; but little did we know it would be homeschooling.

GOOD DOGMA

Why does it take us so long to be truly obedient followers of Jesus? We make progress, but we never reach perfection. Even the rewards of obedience don't keep us on the straight and narrow from dusk to dawn. Jesus promised us joy now and treasures in heaven if we obey him, but we stubbornly refuse to consistently do everything he commands.

You know the story: he tells us to forgive, but sometimes we nurse a grudge. He instructs us to pray, but we neglect prayer. He says, "Fear not," but we worry ourselves to the brink of a breakdown. Yes, we still have a lot to learn. We will be in obedience school for the rest of our lives, but there's good news—our Owner will never give up on us or abandon us.

A BIBLE TREAT

It is God who works in you to will and to act according to his good purpose.
(Phil. 2:13)

12. *Obedience School #3*

AN ARTICLE IN OUR LOCAL NEWSPAPER featured a married couple as a team of dog trainers. They had left their previous professional careers to embark (no pun intended) on a path that would lead owners and their dogs to a loving, happy relationship. The couple specialized in breaking dogs of annoying habits like jumping up on people, charging the front door, engaging in aggressive behavior, and chewing furniture and drapes. And they did the training in their clients' homes.

"Maybe we should give them a call," Gloria offered.

"Okay. Why don't you call them?" I replied. Although the fee was high—higher than a greyhound could leap—we engaged the couple's services.

Ding-dong! They were at our door.

Swoosh, snarl, bark, bark, bark. Molly rushed to engage the enemy!

I held Molly at bay, while the couple leafed through colorful pages of a binder, all designed to explain unacceptable dog behavior and the canine homeschooling remedy. The dog's owners were to assume the lead-dog role and growl loudly, authoritatively at their misbehaving pet. Other behavior-modification techniques accompanied the growling, but the one Gloria and I could not bring ourselves to adopt was the chain-throwing technique. The instructor told us to set a line Molly was not to cross, perhaps ten or fifteen feet from the front door. Throwing a chain in front of Molly if she tried to cross the line was intended to condition her to stop at the line instead of rush to the door.

Throwing a chain worked during the homeschooling session, but once the trainers left, Gloria and I shelved the chain. Not much later, we stopped growling.

Molly had not failed; we had. Consequently, we still had a rush-the-door dog. We decided we could live with one bad habit. We also decided Molly had had enough schooling!

GOOD DOGMA

If my wife and I had taken the tough love approach—the growling and chain throwing—we might have had a perfect dog, but we gave up. Fortunately, God doesn't give up on his children. He lovingly guides our steps, and when we misstep, he convicts us and draws us back to the right way.

Occasionally, we resist his efforts to draw us back. We allow a bad habit to become a behavior. That's when our heavenly Father brings out the chain. He disciplines us when we violate the boundaries of his will. Sometimes the remedy seems harsh, but it is for our good.

A BIBLE TREAT

No discipline seems pleasant at the time, but painful. Later on, however, it produces a harvest of righteousness and peace for those who have been trained by it.

(Heb. 12:11)

13. *Treats Work*

THOSE FREEZE-DRIED, 100 percent pure beef liver treats have endeared me to Molly and to other dogs, too, so I usually carry some in my pocket wherever I go. Although they are odorless, dogs sniff them out and nuzzle up to me, hoping for a handout. "Sit," I tell each begging dog, and sure enough he or she sits. I guess even a dog understands the system of give and take. If it gives obedience, it receives a reward.

It's not that I walk around town like some Santa Claus patron saint of dogs handing out doggy treats indiscriminately, but on my daily walk I often encounter a new four-footed friend who runs to me, having sniffed out my pocketful of treats. And when I am a guest in someone's home, the family dog becomes a friend after just one handout. Even a big aggressive dog in one home turned into a gentle beast when I gave him a treat. (Of course, I always ask an owner's permission before I dole out the goodies.)

Because of the treats, Molly learned early to come when called and to do whatever else I asked. A trainer worth his or her fee will tell you to reduce the handouts gradually and replace them with a pat on the head and a sincere, "Good dog." But being an old softie, I still reward Molly with treats and praise. The treats work. I'm not sure praise without treats would accomplish as much.

Happy dog, happy owner!

GOOD DOGMA

Have you ever thought about God giving us treats? The greatest treat of all is his love. Endless, all encompassing, and unconditional are just a few words that come to mind when I consider his love. The elderly apostle John appreciated God's love. He exclaimed, "How great is the love the Father has lavished on us, that we should be called children of God" (1 John 3:1). He also understood how God's love for us creates a reciprocal love in us. He wrote, "We love because he first loved us" (1 John 4:19).

Peace, joy, confidence, the privilege of prayer, security, guidance, enlightenment, and the fellowship of other believers are additional treats he lavishes on us. How can we help but want to please him, knowing he is so good to us?

A Bible Treat

You have made known to me the path of life; you will fill me with joy in your presence, with eternal pleasures at your right hand.

(Ps. 16:11)

14. Getting My Attention

YOU PROBABLY HAVE a favorite chair you like to relax in for reading and/or watching TV. I do. Mine is a Lazy Boy recliner. My usual position is feet up and head back as far as the chair will go. Sometimes when I am most comfortable, Molly lets me know she wants my attention. I have learned to match her behavior to the kind of attention she wants.

If she needs to go out—or just wants to go out—Molly comes to the left side of the recliner, places her front paws on its left arm, barks twice, and jumps up and down. If that behavior doesn't bring the desired response, she leaps into my lap and stares motionlessly at me. As soon as I ask, "Do you need to go out?" she jumps onto the floor and looks back at me to make sure I got the message.

Molly has another attention-getting strategy. She sits in front of my chair and stares at me. This is her way of saying, "Hey, get out of that chair, lie down on the floor, and play with me." When I oblige, she brings me a ball or some other toy so we can play fetch.

On walks, Molly sometimes signals danger up ahead by stopping, lowering her tail, raising her right paw, and looking straight ahead. This definitely gets my attention, because almost always a big, unleashed dog is waiting to engage us or is approaching us with fire in his eyes.

Occasionally I wonder whether I'm training Molly or she's training me. No big deal—she knows how to get my attention, and I'm glad she does.

Good Dogma

It doesn't take much to get our heavenly Father's attention. He watches over us all the time. He keeps his children as the apple of his eye (Deut. 32:10). When trials and temptations assault us, he makes a way of escape (1 Cor. 10:13). When life's cares lie heavy on our shoulders, he invites us to cast them onto him (Ps. 55:22). And not one anxiety lies beyond his ability to chase it away if we accept his invitation to pray (Phil. 4:6, 7).

We don't have to do cartwheels to catch his attention. We already have it.

The big question is, does God have our attention?

A Bible Treat

I call on you, O God, for you will answer me; give ear to me and hear my prayer.
(Ps. 17:6)

15. Daily Walks

Six months before Molly became a family member, I suffered a stroke. It wasn't a big stroke, but it zapped me big time. Numbness gripped the left corner of my mouth, my left arm, and my left foot. Vicious headaches plagued me day after day after day. Vertigo invaded my equilibrium, duping me into thinking the world was spinning around me. Fatigue subdued me and held me captive. I resigned from the position of senior pastor and wondered when or if I would ever regain enough energy to preach again.

Within a month, most of the numbness disappeared, but the headaches, vertigo, and fatigue were relentless; and I was growing impatient with the endless rounds of medical tests and prescription changes. Then the Lord gave me a live-in therapist—Molly.

I had tried to walk around our block, but it seemed like a marathon without a finish line. Trips with Gloria to the grocery store led me to the nearest bench where I waited for her to complete her purchases. But Molly challenged my lack of mobility. She needed exercise and chose me as her exercise partner.

First, we walked to the end of our street. Then we walked around the block. Next, we ambled to a little park a few blocks away. Finally, we drove to a big park with a two-mile trail. Before long, our daily walks lasted twenty-five minutes at noon and another ten or fifteen minutes in the evening. As our walks progressed, the headaches, vertigo, and fatigue took a hike.

I owe a huge debt of gratitude to the Lord for sending Molly to our home. She may not be a trained rescue dog, but she rescued me from immobility and discouragement.

Good Dogma

A sign in my office says: "Walking is good for the sole." Good observation, but walking with God is even better; it is good for the soul! Enoch would agree. He walked with God in the extremely evil days that preceded the Noahic Flood. Genesis 5:21–24 reports that he maintained his walks with God for three hundred years. According to verse 22, not even the pressures of parenting could keep him from walking with God. As a matter of fact, Enoch never stopped walking with God! Verse 24 states: "Enoch walked with God; then he was no more because God took him away." Over the years, those walks must have been so enjoyable that God decided to catch Enoch up to heaven so the two could continue walking together there.

We, too, can walk with God, and the exercise will make us spiritually strong.

A Bible Treat

He has showed you, O man, what is good. And what does the LORD require of you? To act justly and to love mercy and to walk humbly with your God.

(Mic. 6:8)

16. "Stay!"

I HAD NO TROUBLE getting Molly to follow me. When I walked upstairs, she walked upstairs. When I walked downstairs, she walked downstairs. She was like a little shadow. But would she stay when commanded to do so? I wish I could tell you she obeyed the first time. Truth is, her stay mode lasted about one second—about the time it took me to move one step from her. But gradually, the command to stay took hold.

At first we practiced "Stay!" indoors. As soon as Molly assumed a sit or down position, I placed an open right hand in front of her. A treat in my left hand signaled I would reward obedience. Slowly, I walked a few steps away from her, transferred the treat to my right hand and invited, "Molly, come."

Quickly, Molly was at my feet and eager to receive her reward. Gradually, I increased the distance between us and lengthened the time of the stay.

Next, we moved outdoors where I could put a greater distance between us. Molly could still see me, but it would take longer to reach me. Again, she stayed until I called her.

At dog shows, I have seen trainers command their dogs to assume the stay position, walk somewhere out of their sight, and remain there for ten minutes. The dogs stayed and waited for their masters' return. Frankly, I don't think I could duplicate the feat performed by those trainers. The fault doesn't lie with Molly, but with me. I lack the patience required to train her that thoroughly. Besides, I like having her in sight.

GOOD DOGMA

Before Jesus ascended to heaven, he promised his disciples he would return: "I will come back and take you to be with me that you also may be where I am" (John 14:3). Soon, Jesus was out of sight, and the disciples were on earth in a stay mode. Like obedient dogs, they stood where Jesus had left them. With necks stretched, heads cocked, and eyes riveted on the sky, they watched Jesus depart and must have wondered when he would return. Only the intervention of two angels snapped them out of the stay mode (Acts 1:9–11).

Jesus had not commanded the disciples to simply stay and wait for his return. He had instructed them—and us—to watch and pray and make disciples (Matt. 24:42; 28:18–20). So let's not just sit and wait. Let's work while we wait. If we do the latter, we will receive a reward when he returns from heaven and says, "Come."

A BIBLE TREAT

Behold, I am coming soon! My reward is with me, and I will give to everyone according to what he has done.

(Rev. 22:12)

17. Separation Anxiety

BEING SEPARATED FROM loved ones ranks high on my anxiety scale. The toughest period of life for Gloria and me lasted five years. That's when we lived in the Chicago area from 1990 to 1995—one thousand miles from our three adult children in Denver. We battled separation anxiety daily and counted the days until we reunited with our "kids." When we moved back to Denver, we hoped we had experienced separation for the last time.

We hadn't. It flared up again when I had to put Molly in a kennel so we could participate in the Colorado Christian Writers Conference in Estes Park, Colorado. I drove slowly to "Faithful Friends" kennel all the while telling Molly I had to leave her for a few days, but that she would be okay. When I handed her to the attendant, Molly almost broke my heart. She tried to hide herself in my shoulder and tenaciously held on to me. Separation anxiety must have been dominating her emotions just as it was invading mine.

We returned late Saturday from the conference, but "Faithful Friends" was closed from Saturday noon until 8 a.m. Monday. Guess who was waiting at their doorstep Monday morning?!

GOOD DOGMA

Jesus knew his disciples would experience separation anxiety upon his return to heaven. Therefore, he urged, "Do not let your hearts be troubled" (John 14:1). And he issued a comforting promise, "I will come back."

If you are like most Christians, you get a little weary of living in a world that seems to have gone mad. Terrorism, bedlam, immorality, lawlessness, disrespect, and rising prices cover the face of the globe like warts on a hog's back. You can hardly wait to see Jesus face-to-face. As a hymn suggests, "One glimpse of his dear face all trials will erase." Anxiety separation will end at last.

The big question is: what anxiety do you and I experience when we let a day or two or more separate us from Jesus' spiritual presence? He never leaves us, but we may fail to practice his presence. Fortunately the Holy Spirit stirs us to renew our fellowship with him through confession, prayer, and Bible meditation.

Then we wonder why we ever neglect the opportunity to spend every day with him.

A Bible Treat

They asked each other, "Were not our hearts burning within us while he talked with us on the road and opened the Scriptures to us?"

(Luke 24:32)

18. Unconditional Love

I HAVE TO BE HONEST with you, I sometimes feel sorry for Molly because Gloria and I are age-challenged. We are what society calls "seniors." I'm not fond of the designation, but I can live with it, especially if Gloria and I visit a restaurant that offers a senior discount. However, our senior status means our children are adults. So there are no children living with us. If Molly wants to play, she's stuck with two owners who can get down on the floor, but who take a painfully slow time to get up.

I don't think Molly understands the human aging process. If she does, she has never come right out and barked, "You guys are old and slow." She just accepts us—yes, even loves us—as we are.

When I leave home, Molly follows me to the door and gives me that long look that says, "I'll miss you." When I return, she greets me. She wags her tail, barks, and jumps around my feet. I don't have a dog language translator, but I'm sure she is saying, "I'm glad you're home." If that isn't doggy love, what is?

Yes, sometimes I feel sorry for Molly, and I wish she had kids to play with, but she doesn't seem to fret. She offers unconditional love and shows us that it is real.

GOOD DOGMA

Have you met people who wonder how God can love them? I have. Some have low self-esteem. Others lug a load of guilt around in an unrelenting conscience. Some think God is too busy to care about them because he must spend his time with important matters like making the world go round, keeping the stars lit, managing angels, and restraining powerful evildoers from blowing up the world.

Others believe God's love is limited to those who have gone to church since they were toddlers. A few may be serving time in prison, but how could God possibly love felons?

Well, there is good news. God loves everyone without exception. He loves you and me just as we are. He knows all about our weaknesses, our failures, our blemishes, our imperfections, and our sins. He even knows about our baldness or our big nose or our warts or our freaky big toes; yet he loves us. That's unconditional love, and it's a treasure!

Now, here's an amazing phenomenon. Once we recognize that God loves us unconditionally and we believe on his Son as our Savior, he places his love in our hearts so we can love him and his commandments (Rom. 5:5). The apostle John understood this fact. He wrote, "We love because he first loved us" (1 John 4:19).

A BIBLE TREAT

Very rarely will anyone die for a righteous man. Though for a good man someone might possibly dare to die, but God demonstrates his own love for us in this: While we were yet sinners, Christ died for us.

(Rom. 5:7, 8)

19. Doggy Day Care Treats

I DON'T LEAVE MOLLY at doggy day care very often. It takes a major reason for me to do so. For one thing, Molly doesn't like to be separated from me, even for a few hours. For another, I don't like to be separated from her. Both of us would rather miss the experience.

The ride to doggy care is about as pleasant as a colonoscopy. Since Molly knows the route, she refuses to stay calm in the car. Her agitated pacing and constant whining make me feel like an ogre, and her behavior during check-in makes me feel like an ogre with horns. She buries her face in my shoulder and holds on to me for dear life. I try to erase my guilt by returning early to pick her up.

Perhaps every owner and dog feels the way Molly and I do about doggy day care. I hope not, but the looks I see in the eyes of other owners and dogs confirm my suspicions.

Recently, an owner was checking in his black Lab for the first time. He looked downcast. So did the Lab. I thought he would change his mind, grab his dog by the collar and rush out the door. But he didn't, and the attendant took the Lab to his kennel. When she returned, the owner asked permission to get "a few doggy treats" from his car. She agreed and offered him a small zip-lock bag. "No thanks," he replied as he slipped out the door. Promptly he returned carrying the "few doggy treats"—a twelve-inch-square box of treats and three ten-pound bags of dog food.

Ah, yes, owners and their dogs agree—doggy day care may be necessary, but it is a necessary evil!

GOOD DOGMA

Fifty days after rising from the dead, Jesus ascended to heaven, but first he lifted up his hands and blessed his disciples (Luke 24:50). The physical separation of Jesus from his followers had begun, but he left the first disciples and us with the assurance that he cares. He left his blessing!

Jesus' blessing includes everything we need to survive and thrive until he returns for us. Like the dog owner who left a big box of treats and three huge bags of food for his Lab, Jesus left us an inexhaustible supply of peace, joy, comfort, power, love, grace, mercy, and more. We may be physically separated from him, but we are not separated from his bountiful supply of blessings.

Remember the story of the Good Samaritan? He took a wounded man to an inn and promised the innkeeper: "Look after him, and when I return, I will reimburse you for any extra expense you may have" (Luke 10:35). So Jesus, our Good Samaritan, has written a carte blanche for all we need.

A BIBLE TREAT

And my God will meet all your needs according to his glorious riches in Christ Jesus.

(Phil. 4:19)

20. *Tugging at the Leash*

PUPPIES ARE EITHER BORN with an aversion to the leash or they receive a leash alert from older dogs by mental telepathy. I can't decide whether this aversion is genetic or acquired, but I know it is real and includes the following instructions:

- Hide under a table or chair when owner grabs leash.
- Move your head vigorously from side to side when owner attempts to attach leash to collar.
- Chew on leash and do not lift head.
- Respond to leash by sitting with front paws firmly braced against floor or ground.
- If owner succeeds in pulling you to an upright position, run wildly in circles around owner.
- In case of persistent owner, tug at leash during walk.

Molly followed these instructions to the letter of the law, but finally scrapped them in favor of walking a step or two behind me. Our daily walks have become pleasant and beneficial for both of us. I must confess, though, she still tugs at the leash occasionally. A scent catches her attention now and then, so she yanks the leash to let me know she wants to stop and smell the roses—or something not as fragrant as roses. If she spies a nearby dog or squirrel, she may tug at the leash, apparently hoping I will let her investigate that four-footed wonder.

Perhaps someday we will finish a walk without a single tug at the leash, but for now I'm happy to know Molly ignores the all-points leash alert.

GOOD DOGMA

Our Lord leads us along a narrow way that leads to life everlasting (Matt. 7:14). However, we are not always cooperative. We tug at the leash, preferring to lag behind him or turn aside from him. Sin seems so alluring, so much fun, so exciting! Instead of following the Master closely, occasionally we try to impose our will on him and hope he lets us investigate sights, sounds, and sensations that beckon us away from the narrow path.

The Bible contains stories of believers who tugged at the leash and discovered to their dismay that detours from the narrow way lead to disaster. It also contains stories of those who walked consistently with the Lord and found joy and a deep sense of purpose. The choice is ours.

A BIBLE TREAT

And this is love: that we walk in obedience to his commands. As you have heard from the beginning, his command is that you walk in love.

(2 John 6)

21. Untying Shoestrings

"I'M FROM THE SOUTH," Gloria reminds me when she goes shoeless in the house and yard. Putting on shoes usually means she is going shopping or to church.

Molly has picked up the shoe clue. She is content as long as Gloria traipses around barefoot, but when she dons shoes, Molly launches Operation Shoestrings and attacks Gloria's shoes with the precision of a Patriot Missile. Quicker than you can say Dr. Scholl's®, she unties Gloria's shoestrings. It is simply her way of saying, "You're not going anywhere."

Perhaps the measure is a little drastic, but it's laced with love. Molly loves Gloria so deeply she doesn't want her to leave her. She would gladly hop in the car and accompany Gloria to the grocery store or the mall or Wal-Mart or the Dollar Store, but she would have to sit in the car. Who wants a Maltese on Aisle 11?

Somehow, breakfast cereal and dogs don't go together.

Either Molly will have to stop untying shoestrings or Gloria will have to shop barefoot.

GOOD DOGMA

The man cleansed of demons by Jesus' miraculous power may have considered untying Jesus' sandals. The Bible doesn't report that he did, but it does tell us he implored Jesus to take him with him. Luke 8:38 indicates "the man from whom the demons had gone out begged to go with him [Jesus]." But Jesus turned this man's pleas aside. He commissioned him to "return home and tell how much God has done for you" (v. 38).

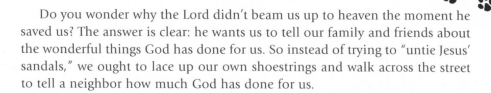

Do you wonder why the Lord didn't beam us up to heaven the moment he saved us? The answer is clear: he wants us to tell our family and friends about the wonderful things God has done for us. So instead of trying to "untie Jesus' sandals," we ought to lace up our own shoestrings and walk across the street to tell a neighbor how much God has done for us.

A BIBLE TREAT

So the man went away and told all over town how much Jesus had done for him.
(Luke 8:39)

22. *Sitting at the Master's Table*

"DON'T LET YOUR DOG come near the table when you are eating. Plan to eat first and then feed your dog. Yadda, yadda, yadda!"

If you can follow these rules, more power to you. I tried, failed, and threw away the training manual. I guess I'm softhearted. My willpower melted the first time Molly looked at me with begging eyes as I stuck my fork into a scrambled egg. She has enjoyed scrambled eggs since that defining moment. I can't share everything I eat with her because it would likely make her ill, but I slip small portions of food to her whenever she sits at my feet and stares at me.

What's her favorite menu? Eggs, beef, bacon, cottage cheese, Swiss cheese, and ice cream. Since she is a Maltese, she would probably prefer a Mediterranean diet, but I wouldn't. So she will have to be content with my food choices.

GOOD DOGMA

King David wanted to show kindness to former King Saul's family members. Saul had tried to kill David, but Saul's son, Jonathan, had befriended David and even saved his life. Now both Saul and Jonathan were dead, victims of a fierce assault by Israel's archenemy, the Philistines.

But David learned that Jonathan had a crippled son, Mephibosheth, who was living in a desolate place. Apparently, Mephibosheth was hiding from David. He must have thought David would take revenge on him because his grandfather, Saul, had tried to kill David. But David had kindness—not killing—on his mind, and he dispatched a servant to bring Mephibosheth to the palace.

Second Samuel 9 tells what happened next.

When Mephibosheth entered David's presence, he bowed low and asked David, "What is your servant, that you should notice a dead dog like me?" (v. 8). David responded by giving Mephibosheth property, servants, and the privilege of eating at the king's table as one of his own sons (v. 9–13).

What David did for Mephibosheth demonstrates what Jesus, the King of kings, has done for believers. He has showered his kindness on us by bringing us from a desolate place in life to him. He has graced us with gifts and a title deed to a mansion in heaven, and he allows us to "sit at his table" where we fellowship with him daily and feast on his Word.

Give thanks today for all good things you enjoy at the Master's table!

A Bible Treat

He has taken me to the banquet hall, and his banner over me is love.

(Song of Sol. 2:4)

23. *Where He Leads Me*

SOME DOGS RIDE WELL IN A CAR; others don't. Molly is in the first category. As soon as I open the car door she jumps in as if to say, "Let's roll!" And when we roll, she usually curls up in the passenger seat, only interrupting her rest occasionally to peak out the window. She seems perfectly content to leave the destination and route to me.

A couple of exceptions come into play. Molly has a built-in GPS. She has identified certain streets as high-stress thoroughfares and becomes agitated when I drive on them. She has learned that one set of streets leads to the vet's office, and the whimper turns to anguished cries as we near the vet's office.

Another set of streets produce ambivalent feelings. They lead to the park where we enjoy leisurely strolls. But doggy day care lies a mile past the park. As we approach the park, Molly looks out the passenger window. She remains quiet but alert, likely hoping we will pull into the park's parking lot. However, if we drive past the park, she grows antsy. She knows our destination is doggy day care, not the park. Soon, she lets me know with whimpers and cries how she feels about what lies ahead.

I would never cause Molly any discomfort if I could avoid it, but trips to the vet are for her good. Also, doggy day care is unavoidable at times, and whether she realizes it or not, I would never abandon her. I tell her everything will be okay, but only the passing of time reassures her.

Good Dogma

I think our churches lost something when they switched from hymnbooks to choruses projected onto a screen. Many old hymns and gospel songs remind us that the Christian life is a walk of faith. One of my favorites is "Where He Leads Me I Will Follow." The last part of the chorus reads, "I'll go with him, with him all the way."

We may not know where our Savior is leading us, but following him all the way always leads to what is best for us. So we go with him, all the way.

Hebrews 11:8 memorializes Abraham's faith because when God called him to leave his homeland, Abraham "obeyed, and went, even though he didn't know where he was going." Sometimes, God led Abraham through difficult circumstances, like the time he asked him to offer his son Isaac as a burnt offering. But God also rewarded Abraham's faith and called him his friend (James 2:23).

We can whimper, whine, cry, and get antsy when life's roads lead to discomfort or loneliness, but knowing the Lord has designed everything and every place for our good, we can also trust him and "enjoy the ride."

A Bible Treat

If I rise on the wings of the dawn, if I settle on the far side of the sea, even there your hand will guide me, your right hand will hold me fast.

(Ps. 139:9, 10)

24. *First Thing Every Morning*

AFTER BREAKFAST AND BEFORE starting the workday, I grab a cup of coffee, relax in my recliner, and read the morning paper. Molly sits at my feet and watches until I open the paper. She views the paper opening as the signal for her to jump onto my lap, where she curls up until I come to the classifieds. When I toss the classifieds aside, she jumps down and waits for me to walk upstairs to my home office.

Molly and the newspaper clashed when she was a puppy. When she jumped into my lap in those early days, she must have thought the paper was competing with her for my attention. She clawed and chewed the paper until it was shredded writ. What a contrast between her puppy behavior and her behavior now!

I don't think I would enjoy coffee and the newspaper nearly so much if Molly weren't on my lap. I don't read the headlines to her or show her the cartoons, but the quiet, peaceful time we spend together is worth the quarterly subscription.

GOOD DOGMA

Unless you live on a deserted island far from civilization, you lead a hurry-scurry, hustle and bustle life. Frequently you may feel like yelling, "Stop the world, I want to get off." Perhaps you have gone camping to get away from it all, only to check into a crowded campground crammed with frenetic strangers who are also trying to get away from it all.

Even a hospital stay (not recommended as an escape to solitude) can be anything but quiet. Ironic, isn't it, that street signs caution, "Quiet. Hospital Zone," but little or no rest awaits the patients inside. If you fall asleep in a hospital bed, you can be sure nurses will wake you several times during the night to check vital signs and administer medication. Or, even worse, a long-needle shot will jolt you into sudden consciousness!

After a few days of the middle-of-the-night "health care" and daytime noisy visitors, you can hardly wait to get home for a rest.

We all need quality quiet time, and the best quiet time consists of a daily one-on-one meeting with Jesus. Two sisters, Martha and Mary, entertained Jesus in their home. Mary sat at Jesus' feet, "listening to what he said" (Luke 10:39), but Martha scurried about, "distracted by all the preparations that had to be made" (v. 40).

Jesus commented on the sisters' contrasting behaviors. "You are worried and upset about many things, but only one thing is needed," he told Martha. Commending Mary's behavior, he said, "Mary has chosen what is better" (v. 41).

Each day brings many choices, but the best choice is quiet time with Jesus.

A BIBLE TREAT

In the morning, O LORD, you hear my voice; in the morning I lay my requests before you and wait in expectation.

(Ps. 5:3)

25. Catching Some ZZZZs

THE FIRST NIGHT AWAY from Mamma, Molly was restless. We could tell from her crying that she felt insecure about her new surroundings. However, the second night she slept soundly and didn't wake up until we did. That good sleep pattern has continued with the exception of a few nights when an upset tummy interrupted her sleep.

She must not have a guilty conscience or feel anxious about a possible bad hair day at the groomer's, because she takes a long afternoon nap after we walk a mile or two. Again, in the evening she retreats to her bed for a siesta. When she is awake, she is ready to play. When she decides to sleep, neither doggy toy nor biscuit can keep her from her zzzzs.

There must be a reason for the saying, "Let sleeping dogs lie." I don't intend to challenge it.

GOOD DOGMA

Sleep is vital to our health. It restores energy, calms the mind, soothes aches and pains, and helps us stay alert, productive, and creative. It may also contribute to our spiritual well-being. Sure, our light will shine brighter if we burn it at both ends, but it will go out sooner.

Elijah burned the candle at both ends. On Mount Carmel he had engaged 450 prophets of Baal in an all-day contest to decide who was truly God. At the end of the day, he ordered the execution of those false prophets.

From Mount Carmel, he ran about twenty-five miles to Jezreel. Then, after receiving a death threat from Queen Jezebel, he traveled through Israel and Judah and went a day's journey into the Negev Desert. Finding the shade of a desert bush, he plopped down and finally fell asleep.

Elijah in the desert was hardly the same man as Elijah on the mountain. In the desert he was distraught and discouraged, lacking neither confidence in God nor the will to live. Sleep was an essential step to revival in his life. The Lord let him sleep and then guided him through the remaining steps to revival.

A friend used to say, "Christians on their way to heaven should be in bed by eleven." He may have been on to something!

A Bible Treat

I will lie down and sleep in peace, for you alone, O LORD, make me dwell in safety.

(Ps. 4:8)

26. A Thorn in the Paw

THE HIGHLINE CANAL SNAKES it way through Littleton, Colorado, and draws residents to its cottonwood-lined banks for a hike or leisurely stroll. Coloradans call it a canal, but midwesterners and easterners would call it a ditch. After all, it is quite narrow and rarely has any water. So it is a safe place to walk with small children or dogs.

Molly and I hiked the Highline Canal trail one beautiful fall day alongside the Highlands Ranch Golf Course. Being an avid golfer, I used the occasion to saunter off the trail and into the rough in search of lost golf balls. Molly tagged along behind me—jauntily at first, but then haltingly. When she stopped walking, I thought she was tired, but then I discovered a thorn in her right front paw.

Guilt overwhelmed me. Why had I ventured off the trail and taken Molly into an area of spindly grass, yucca, thistles, cacti, and other prickly weeds? Even if I had found a hundred Titleist golf balls, they would not have compensated for Molly's injury. The best I could do at the moment was console her, pick her up, and carry her the long mile back to our origination—my daughter's and son-in-law's house where tweezers would remove the thorn.

The walk back to the house taught me a few things: (1) Molly was heavier than I expected; (2) my back was weaker than I expected; (3) golf balls hit into the rough should stay where they land; and (4) I would never lead Molly astray again.

GOOD DOGMA

Unlike a dog on a leash, every human being has chosen to stray from God and walk in sin (Isa. 53:6). As a result of that choice, we inflicted great harm on ourselves. But Jesus, the Good Shepherd, launched a search and rescue mission on our behalf. Upon finding us, he picked us up and carried us home (Luke 15:1–5).

Now, as his followers, we can walk with Jesus anywhere. He never leads us astray. The path may seem rough at times, but he never lets anything harm us. Let's enjoy the walk!

A BIBLE TREAT

When he [the Good Shepherd] has brought out all his own, he goes on ahead of them, and his sheep follow him because they know his voice.

(John 10:4)

27. "No Bark!"

As I MENTIONED EARLIER, a dog trainer advised Gloria and me to throw a small chain in front of Molly when she barked. I guess the idea was to scare her into silence. Does a frightened dog bark less?

To be honest with you, I confess I tossed the chain in front of Molly a couple of times, but doing so just didn't feel right. *How would I like it if somebody threw a chain in my direction?* I wondered. So I put the chain away, and I have no idea where I stashed it. I simply remember that I was the weakest link in the anti-barking training technique.

The barking continued whenever anyone approached our front door or even walked past our house. But instead of looking for the chain, I dropped some serious dollars in a pet store in exchange for a shock collar. The instructions that accompanied the collar said a low setting would deliver a very mild and harmless shock. So I mustered the courage to give it a whirl.

Even the second lowest setting jolted Molly so strongly that she yelped and recoiled. That was enough of that, I decided, and I apologized to Molly as I shelved the collar.

What finally worked was a simple voice command. It didn't catch on immediately, but gradually "No bark" was the most effective deterrent ever. Eventually she abandoned the barking habit on command.

GOOD DOGMA

Do you ever find yourself "barking" about life's unfairness or others' irritating behavior? The barking usually starts with a grumble and a growl. We complain in low angry tones that God must not care about us because if he cared, we reason, he would have prevented the car accident. If he really loved us, we would not have lost our job or broken an arm or spilled gravy on the white linen tablecloth.

We growl about Gus's eternally long announcement in last Sunday's church service or the youth pastor's failure to provide activities for the young teens. Soon, the growling gives way to barking. Our family members and friends become annoyed with our loud complaining about anything and everything from the way the President is conducting the war on terrorism to the way the church's music director is conducting the choir.

We know the barking has to stop. But how?

We don't need someone to throw a chain at us. Nor would we welcome a mild shock. The best way to stop our barking is to heed God's voice command, given in Ephesians 4:31: "Get rid of all bitterness, rage and anger, brawling and slander, along with every form of malice."

A BIBLE TREAT

Do not let any unwholesome talk come out of your mouths, but only what is helpful for building others up according to their needs, that it may benefit those who listen.

(Eph. 4:29)

28. SSSSSurprise!

EMBARKING ON A SUNNY afternoon walk, Molly and I passed our neighbor's house and rounded the corner where a surprise awaited us. A rattlesnake coiled up on the sidewalk appeared ready to challenge our use of its place in the sun. I had heard long-time Colorado Springs residents refer to my neighborhood of new homes as "rattlesnake hill." Suddenly, I realized they knew what they were talking about.

Recently, a neighbor had found a rattlesnake near his window well, and another had discovered one in the shrubs at the front of his house. Now, Molly and I had stumbled onto one.

A faint rattle persuaded me to keep Molly from investigating our neighborhood's uninvited guest. I backed up slowly, and Molly followed. We crossed the street and continued on our way. By the time we returned, the rattler had left.

GOOD DOGMA

The Bible identifies the devil as "that ancient serpent" (Rev. 20:2). The devil first made his appearance in human history in the Garden of Eden, where he assumed the form of a serpent. His goal then was to dupe Eve and detract Adam from God's will. He succeeded. Adam and Eve fell into sin, and the human race has suffered moral and spiritual disaster from that day until now.

We can't pin all the blame on Adam and Eve, though. We may lament, "If only Eve had walked away from the serpent at its first hiss. If only Adam had not eaten the forbidden fruit when Eve handed it to him." But, let's be honest, we have all sinned. Instead of fleeing from the serpent, we have fallen for his tempting lies.

If it were not for the fact that Jesus defeated the serpent by dying for our sins, we would be doomed to hear his hiss at close range throughout eternity.

When the devil confronts us on our walk through life, we ought to walk away, avoid him, and follow our Master.

A BIBLE TREAT

The great dragon was hurled down—that ancient serpent called the devil, or Satan, who leads the world astray. He was hurled to the earth, and his angels with him. Then I heard a loud voice in heaven say: "Now have come the salvation and the power and the kingdom of our God, and the authority of his Christ. For the accuser of our brothers, who accuses them before our God day and night, has been hurled down."

(Rev. 12:9, 10)

29. A New Look

I READ A PAMPHLET in the vet's office that claims grooming makes dogs feel better. The theory may be that less hair or at least less matted hair makes Fido feel more comfortable. Frankly, when I leave a barbershop, I don't feel any better. I don't have much hair to begin with, and I kind of resent a barber's clipping away the little I do have. Paying him to do so only adds insult to injury!

Unlike me, Molly has lots of hair. If we didn't groom her regularly, her hair would flow long like the Nile or become matted like a bramble bush. So every five weeks or so, Molly goes to the groomer. She doesn't like me handing her over to the groomer. She grabs my shoulder and hangs on for dear life before I leave her. However, when I pick her up from the groomer, I can tell she is well pleased with her new look. She parades around the house with a happy bounce.

I'm sure money spent for grooming Molly is a much better expenditure than money spent on me at the barbershop.

GOOD DOGMA

Some preachers claim that a person looks different when he or she becomes a Christian. "His face glow now," I have heard them say.

Frankly, I have never seen a man's face glow unless he was standing under a high-wattage light. Nor have I seen a woman's face glow unless she had applied too much moisturizing cream.

But Christians' lives ought to look different from those of unbelievers. Indeed, the Scriptures command us to put off old sinful habits and put on qualities that accent our new life in Christ. Ephesians 4:24–32 instructs us to put off falsehood, resentment, stealing, indolence, unwholesome talk, bitterness, rage and anger, brawling, and slander, and every form of malice.

Our new look should display righteousness, holiness, truth, reasonableness, honesty, industry, constructive talk, sensitivity to the Spirit, kindness, compassion, and forgiveness. Perhaps we should look into the mirror of God's Word today and see how well we are displaying a new look.

A Bible Treat

But the man who looks intently into the perfect law that gives freedom, and continues to do this, not forgetting what he has heard, but doing it—he will be blessed in what he does.

(James 1:25)

30. Good Dogs—Bad Dogs

IF YOU WALK YOUR DOG REGULARLY, you know the world of dogs falls into two categories—good dogs and bad dogs—although it might be more accurate to say good owners and bad owners. Good owners train their dogs to behave appropriately, and they keep them on a leash. Bad owners allow dogs to behave inappropriately. When you encounter a bad dog, you fear it will attack your dog or you or both.

Molly was about six months old when a stroll in our neighborhood park turned ugly. I noticed a man and a big dog were playing fetch on the far side of the park. Although the dog wasn't on a leash, it seemed to be under control. The owner would toss a tennis ball about thirty yards, and the dog would obediently retrieve it.

Suddenly, the dog saw Molly, dropped the tennis ball, and came bounding across the field. I stood still, but when the dog came close, I felt Molly's leash slacken. Molly had slipped out of the collar and was bolting across the park, zigzagging with the big dog in hot pursuit.

I watched helplessly and anxiously as Molly and the "villain" raced round and round the park. I feared Molly would leave the park and run into traffic, but she didn't. Fortunately, she kept circling back to me at breakneck speed. But because her pursuer was at her heels, she didn't break stride when she reached me.

Finally, on one of the turns, I caught her and held her high. The chase dog was jumping up at Molly when her owner approached and grabbed his dog. He apologized, and I accepted his apology, but suggested the incident would not have occurred if he had kept his dog on a leash.

Most dogs in the park are friendly, as are their owners, but in a fallen world, there will always be bad dogs as well as good dogs. After learning that lesson, I tightened Molly's collar and resolved to stay alert.

GOOD DOGMA

Jesus taught us to "watch out for false prophets." He explained that they may look harmless, but they are vicious deceivers. "They come to you in sheep's clothing, but inwardly they are ferocious wolves," he said (Matt. 5:15). These "bad" religious leaders chase the unsuspecting and, if they catch them, destroy their faith.

The apostle Paul urged the Christians at Philippi to stay alert to attacks by "bad" religious leaders. He called them "dogs," and warned, "Watch out for those dogs, those men who do evil" (Phil. 3:2).

How can we protect ourselves from false prophets? If we become familiar with God's Word, we will recognize error and the evil designs of those who teach error. The psalmist expressed this truth in the words: "Because I love your commands more than gold, more than our gold, and because I consider all your precepts right, I hate every wrong path" (Ps. 119:127, 128).

A BIBLE TREAT

Great peace have they who love your law, and nothing can make them stumble.
(Ps. 119:165)

31. Nimmy Nose

GLORIA CALLS MOLLY "Nimmy Nose." I think it's a name she picked up from her paternal grandmother to describe a highly inquisitive, perhaps even nosy, person. The name fits Molly perfectly.

I know all dogs poke their noses into all kinds of objects, some of which I don't have to identify for you. Their legs follow their sniffers as eagerly as kids follow an ice cream truck. But Molly sticks her nose into so many things I have to wonder if a bloodhound slipped undetected into her lineage. Whatever enters our house undergoes the Nimmy Nose inspection. Whether it's a new recliner or a new addition to Gloria's doll collection, it receives a Nimmy Nose sniffing from top to bottom and from side to side.

Gloria's crocheting supplies seem to be under long-term investigation as daily Molly pokes her nose into the supply basket and emerges with yarn she proceeds to unravel and sniff.

Nimmy Nose investigates pockets and purses, too. We have to caution our guests about this habit, otherwise they may find a Maltese investigator rummaging through a pocket or purse. Maybe Molly just wants to check one or two photo IDs for security reasons.

If someone should ever post a reward in our neighborhood for a lost diamond ring, I plan to launch "Operation Nimmy Nose."

GOOD DOGMA

The Bible censures busybodies, but it encourages us to be inquisitive students of truth. Solomon searched diligently for truth, nimmy-nosing his way along a path that led only to frustration and emptiness of heart until he discovered the meaning of life in a relationship with God. He wrote in Ecclesiastes 1:13, 14: "I devoted myself to study and to explore by wisdom all that is done under heaven. . . . I have seen all the things that are done under the sun; all of them are meaningless, a chasing after the wind." He concluded, "Remember your Creator in the days of your youth" (12:1).

The Christians at Berea followed a nimmy-nose approach to truth. Acts 17:11 reports that they "examined the Scriptures every day to see if what Paul said was true."

Sticking our noses into God's Word every day is a good habit. As we read the Bible, we ought to search for truths about God, others, and ourselves. We should ferret out promises to claim, commands to obey, prayers to offer, sins to avoid, and examples to follow. God will bless our lives and be pleased.

A BIBLE TREAT

Open my eyes that I may see wonderful things in your law.

(Ps. 119:18)

32. The Future Is in the Master's Hands

TWO DAYS AFTER WRITING this devotional book, I planned to drop Molly off at doggy day care. Gloria and I would be spending the day in Denver, seventy miles north of our home in Colorado Springs. I also planned to take Molly to the Sunnyside Veterinarian Clinic for routine shots a couple of months later. She won't enjoy either trip, but both trips are for her good. If she knew what the future held, she would surely fret and whine now. Of course, I can't guarantee that my plans for two days from now or two months from now will come to pass, but I can plan ahead and anticipate that everything will go as scheduled.

Molly doesn't seem to be anxious about the future. Maybe dogs are naturally more trusting than people. As far as I can tell, she doesn't worry about tomorrow's food or water or whether she will have a roof over her head. She lets me take care of all those matters.

GOOD DOGMA

More than a few times I have acted as though my life's motto was, "Why pray when you can worry?" When a rare and aggressive cancer appeared on my left ear, my doctor recommended early and aggressive surgery. He explained that it was a fast-growing cancer that could spread quickly to the lymph system. Also, he warned that it could recur after surgery and might require five successive surgeries to get rid of it. Finally, he told me if I had gone another month without surgery, I would have lost the ear to cancer.

I worried that I might become a modern-day Van Gogh, but one without a grain of artistic ability. I worried I might die and leave my wife in financial difficulty.

I worried I would look weird with part of my ear missing. To say my faith was challenged would be an understatement. It was bombarded. But what little faith I had, I placed in the Lord, and he brought me safely through the trial.

I have faced other health challenges since the ear surgery, and I think I am learning to place my future in the Lord's hands. Nothing placed in his hands falls through his fingers. He holds not only the future but also all who commit the future to his care.

A BIBLE TREAT

Do not be anxious about anything. But in everything by prayer and petition, with thanksgiving, present your requests to God. And the peace of God, which transcends all understanding, will guard your hearts and your minds in Christ Jesus."

(Phil. 4:6, 7)

33. *Sisterly Love*

IF ONE DOG IS GOOD, two must be better. Molly had become such a loving member of our family that we decided to get another dog. Molly had grown much more attached to me than to Gloria, so why not get a puppy she could dote over and call her dog?

Rosie, a red toy poodle, entered our home when Molly was a year old. They hit it off immediately, and so did Gloria and Rosie.

Rosie followed Molly around like a little girl follows an older sister. To this day they play together, eat together, walk together, often sit together in a recliner, and even fall asleep together in front of the fireplace on a big doggie pillow. Early evening seems to be their favorite time for hide-and-seek.

The game begins when they crouch down and stare at each other. Rosie's bark signals the start of the game, and they are off and running in the family room. Rosie runs behind the TV, sticks her head out from one side, but quickly bolts to the back of a chair when Molly gives chase. Eventually, Rosie hides under the sofa. When her nose appears under the sofa skirt, Molly jumps at her, and she retreats, only to pop her nose out at another spot.

Perhaps the most endearing scene is that of Rosie and Molly lying together in the same crate at the end of the day. They are sisters indeed!

GOOD DOGMA

Two women in the Philippian church were embroiled in a spat. We don't know the issue that put them at odds with each other, and perhaps they didn't

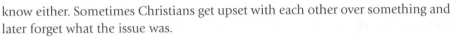

know either. Sometimes Christians get upset with each other over something and later forget what the issue was.

They also forget that the Bible teaches Christians to love and to forgive one another (Eph. 4:32; 5:2). They simply remember that they are at odds. At any rate, Paul addressed these two feuding females, Euodia and Syntyche, and urged them to "agree with each other in the Lord" (Phil. 4:2).

Both women had contributed much to the cause of Christ, and Paul did not want to see their disagreement mar their record of Christian service (v. 3).

Sisters and brothers in Christ ought to love one another and agree to disagree agreeably when they do not see eye to eye. An occasional spat doesn't have to escalate into a war of words; it can end quickly when love establishes peace. Jesus said the world would know we are his by our love (John 13:35).

A BIBLE TREAT

How good and pleasant it is when brothers [and sisters] live together in unity.
(Ps. 133:1)

A BUMPER STICKER ANNOUNCES: "My border collie is smarter than your honor student!"

Is this an exaggerated claim? Of course, but let's not shortchange our four-legged best friends. They are smart. At least, my dog is smart. Her understanding of my commands and instructions amaze me. I can say, "Molly, bring me a ball," and she brings me a ball. If I tell her to bring me a shoe or a toy, she brings the right item. If I throw a ball behind a recliner while she isn't watching, I can point and say, "Molly, your ball is behind that chair." Promptly, she jaunts to the chair, walks behind it, and emerges with the ball.

Perhaps the most startling display of Molly's intelligence occurred one day when I called her and Rosie in from the backyard. She responded to my call, but Rosie ignored it. I called a few more times, but still Rosie dillydallied in the yard. Frustrated, I said, "Molly, tell Rosie to get in here." Molly trotted out to the deck, looked out at Rosie, and barked authoritatively. Immediately and in high gear, Rosie came running into the house.

If a dog's authoritative bark elicited a similar response in humans, likely wives all across America would be using them to summon their husbands!

GOOD DOGMA

God endowed his people with spiritual intelligence, a wisdom that unbelievers do not possess. It is the ability to understand God's commands and instructions and apply them to daily life. The apostle Paul credited this wisdom to the presence and ministry of the Holy Spirit. He wrote, "No one knows the thoughts of

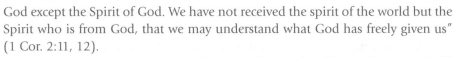

God except the Spirit of God. We have not received the spirit of the world but the Spirit who is from God, that we may understand what God has freely given us" (1 Cor. 2:11, 12).

Our associates may question righteous behavior that flies in the face of self-centeredness and sinful pleasure, but we are simply responding to the commands and instructions of our Master. It's far better to please him than to give in to the dictates of a dog-eat-dog world.

A BIBLE TREAT

For this reason, since the day we heard about you, we have not stopped praying for you, and asking God to fill you with the knowledge of his will through all spiritual wisdom and understanding."

(Col. 1:9)

35. *Too Quiet*

BEING A WELL-MANNERED DOG, Molly refuses to walk ahead of me. She follows at my heels. She waits for me to walk through a doorway and then follows. When I get out of the car, she hops out and waits for me to lead her. She doesn't climb a stairway until my foot lands on the first step; then she tags behind.

Occasionally, Molly has followed me without me being aware of her doing so. That has presented a problem. For instance, occasionally I go to the basement in search of just the right book amidst hundreds of books stashed there, or I walk into the garage to find a hammer or a screwdriver. Upon leaving the basement or garage, I close the door to the living area. A few minutes later it dawns on me Molly isn't with me.

"Molly, come," I call. "Where are you, Molly?"

No answer! I search high and low for her. I don't find her in my office or curled up on a bed or napping in her crate or resting on the sun porch. Panic begins to set in. I yell, "Molly!"

No answer! I scour the fenced backyard without finding her. Finally, I remember having gone to the basement or the garage. So I open the door and discover Molly sitting quietly behind it. Sometimes she is too quiet!

GOOD DOGMA

It seems to me that often Christians are too quiet when we should let others hear our voices. We need to call upon the Lord at all times. When we fall into temptation or wander from the safety of fellowship with the Lord, we need to cry out to him for deliverance.

The Lord predicted that at the close of the Babylonian Captivity the exiled Jews would "call upon me and come and pray to me" (Jer. 29:12). He promised, "I will listen to you. You will seek me and find me when you seek me with all your heart" (vv. 12, 13).

Trouble drives us to pray.

We should also refuse to remain quiet about the widespread disregard for moral and spiritual values. Why hold our peace when the values that made our nation strong are under attack? A well-crafted, diplomatic letter to an editor may help retard the decline and even influence others to turn to the Lord.

Sometimes silence isn't golden; it's just plain yellow.

A BIBLE TREAT

Shout aloud and sing for joy, people of Zion, for great is the Holy One of Israel among you.

(Isa. 12:6)

36. *Rejected—Ejected*

ANNUALLY, AT THE END OF MAY, Old Colorado City, a small town near the base of Pike's Peak, celebrates Territory Days. The three-day event honors the town as the first capital of the Colorado Territory. Authorities block off several blocks of Colorado Avenue, the main street, while craft booths and lunch stands line both sides of the street. Crowds meander along, peering into one craft booth after another. Vendors offer anything from a turquoise bracelet to an oak shelf, and patrons can sink their teeth into anything from a buffalo burger to a bratwurst and wash it down with hot coffee, soda, or ice-cold lemonade.

Because the Territory Days celebration draws huge crowds and parking isn't available on the main street, finding a parking spot blocks away is reason alone to celebrate. Gloria and I almost jumped for joy when we found one. With our two little dogs on their leashes, we were happy campers as we promenaded several blocks to the main street. But then something happened that changed our mood dramatically.

"Sir, dogs are not allowed here." I turned to find a deputy sheriff staring at Gloria and me.

"Let them stay," a vendor called. "Their cute dogs have drawn a crowd to my booth."

"Sorry," the deputy sheriff intoned. "They will have to leave."

Rejected and ejected, we led Molly and Rosie to our car and drove home.

GOOD DOGMA

Rejection feels awful. If you have experienced it, you know that awful feeling. You feel unwanted, unacceptable, even despised. You just want to find a quiet place to sulk and lick your wounds. You may nurse resentment.

Jesus experienced rejection. He came into the world to save the lost, but the human race despised and rejected him (Isa. 53:3; John 1:11). During the Jewish Passover celebration, soldiers arrested Jesus, and the religious authorities subjected him to an illegal, all-night trial and mockery. Governor Pilate had him beaten and gave a bloodthirsty crowd the opportunity to decide whether to release Jesus or crucify him.

"Crucify him!" they shouted. Soldiers led Jesus out of Jerusalem (he was ejected from the Holy City), nailed him to a cross, and watched him die.

Jesus did not deserve rejection and crucifixion, but he willingly endured both for our sake. Because he chose to suffer for our sins, we can celebrate because God has accepted us into his family forever.

A BIBLE TREAT

All that the Father gives me will come to me, and whoever comes to me I will never drive away.

(John 6:37)

37. Keeping Toys in Their Place

A CORNER OF OUR FAMILY ROOM is a repository for dog toys. Some lie in an open box; others cover a small area around the box. Most of them squeak, but a few do absolutely nothing. The cache includes taut rope, balls on ropes, balls without ropes, bells on rope, toy bones of various sizes, stuffed animals, toy shoes, and even a rubber foot with painted toenails. Rosie's favorites are a soft ball about the size of a tennis ball and a tiny stuffed lion. Molly's uncontested favorite is a laced red and white athletic shoe.

Most evenings, Molly and Rosie dig around in their toys until they select one to bring to me. They expect me to toss it across the room for them to chase and fetch. Occasionally, they compete to see which of them carries it all the way back to me. Often, they bring it to me in tandem. Molly grips one side of the toy with her teeth, and Rosie grips the other side. Low growling indicates their displeasure with the compromise.

Taking the toy from them, I ask, "Are you ready?" They signal their readiness to fetch by sitting quietly and looking up at me. Then I throw the toy, and the chase to retrieve it is under way.

Who can explain Molly's and Rosie's choice of toys? Once in a while, they rummage through the toy cache and select a toy I have long forgotten—like the rubber foot. Regardless of their preferences, they seem to understand that there is a place for toys and how to place them in their master's hands.

Good Dogma

A popular bumper sticker reads: THE GUY WHO DIES WITH THE MOST TOYS WINS!

Obviously, whoever dreamed up the bumper sticker doesn't understand that "toys"—cars, boats, TVs, golf clubs, electronic gadgets, stereos, and collectors' items—are just things. If we keep them in their place, they can entertain us or make life easier or more pleasant. But "things" can blight our lives if we do not place them in the Master's hands.

Jesus warned us, "Watch out! Be on your guard against all kinds of greed," explaining that, "a man's life does not consist in the abundance of his possessions" (Luke 12:15).

Allegedly, when Alexander the Great was dying, he requested to be buried with his hands open, showing that he had taken nothing into the afterlife.

Perhaps a more accurate bumper sticker message should read: HE WHO DIES WITH NOTHING BUT TOYS—LOSES.

A Bible Treat

But store up for yourselves treasures in heaven, where moth and rust do not destroy, and where thieves do not break in and steal.

(Matt. 6:20)

38. *Little Birds and Little Dogs*

AH, SPRING, WHEN LITTLE BOYS try out their batting swing and little birds try out their wings!

Spring graced our backyard ponderosa pine with a family of robins—a mother, a father, and three babies. Their nest was barely visible, tucked behind tangled branches, up high and near the trunk. But Mama Robin couldn't hide her frequent flights to the nest as she carried worms to her little ones. Soon, she enrolled them in flight school, and backyard activity reached a fever pitch.

Occasionally, the baby robins fell to the ground not far from their nest, flapping their wings, but failing to achieve liftoff. Their spirited chirping and fluttering attracted Molly and Rosie who rushed to them.

At first I feared my two little dogs would maim or kill the baby birds. Mama Robin must have shared my fear. From a nearby fence, she nose-dived at Molly and Rosie, swooped over their heads, returned to the fence and repeated the maneuver. But Molly and Rosie simply sniffed the birds and followed them, noses to tails, as they went bob-bob-bobbing along.

After corralling Molly and Rosie, I picked up each bird and placed it back into the nest. All the while Mama Robin watched alertly. I hope she understood my little dogs were just exercising canine curiosity and intended no harm.

GOOD DOGMA

We can see our heavenly Father's limitless power and wisdom in the vast complexity of the universe. Astronomers are still discovering planets and stars

God spoke into existence "in the beginning." But our heavenly Father is also providential and caring.

Jesus observed, "Are not two sparrows sold for a penny? Yet not one of them will fall to the ground apart from the will of your Father" (Matt. 10:29). Jesus drew a satisfying comparison between our heavenly Father's concern for a sparrow and his care of us. He has numbered even the hairs of our head and values each of us highly. Why then, should we worry? Our heavenly Father watches over us.

A BIBLE TREAT

And even the very hairs of your head are all numbered. So don't be afraid; you are worth more than many sparrows.

(Matt. 10:30, 31)

39. *Siesta Time*

MOLLY AND ROSIE PLAY HARD, but they never skip their siestas. After lunch they follow me upstairs to my office and take their positions for a refreshing nap. Molly curls up on a doggie pillow beside my workstation, while Rosie claims her spot under my computer desk or in my lap. Perhaps the tap, tap, tap of my computer keyboard lulls them to sleep. Or could their sleepiness be a subtle commentary on the quality of my writing? At any rate, daily resting has become a habit.

When they wake, they stretch and are ready to go for a walk, engage in playful wrestling or initiate a game of chase. Apparently, unlike human beings, they don't need anyone to convince them that rest is necessary to sustain good health and vitality.

GOOD DOGMA

A busy pastor kept a sign in his office: BEWARE OF THE BARRENNESS OF A BUSY LIFE.

Perhaps you and I need such a sign. We live in a frantic-paced world and in spite of time-saving devices, we don't seem to accomplish half the tasks listed in our day timers. We hurry from meeting to meeting or from place to place because of a tight schedule. We hurry to fix dinner or to eat out, and then we hurry to catch up on our e-mail correspondences or to finish reading the paper that lies open beside an unfinished cup of coffee. Maybe we are slowly shortening our lives by hurry-scurry.

Remember what Jesus said to his disciples, "Come with me to a quiet place and get some rest"? His words convict us, and we have to adjust our priorities. Instead of running on a treadmill of ceaseless activities, we need to step off and spend some quiet time with Jesus. Doing so will restore energy to our souls and revitalize our fellowship with him.

Spiritual siestas may be the best answer to an overcrowded schedule!

A BIBLE TREAT

Be still before the LORD and wait patiently for him.

(*Ps. 37:7*)

40. Kid Safe

SOME TOYS AND STUFFED ANIMALS may not be kid safe. Little children can easily choke on a small toy or toy part or a stuffed animal's button nose or eyes. Dogs, too, may not be kid safe. If they have had minimal or no exposure to little children, dogs may become startled and bite when little hands reach for them or fingers poke them. So it is wise to give dogs lots of opportunities to socialize with children beginning in the puppy stage.

From the time Molly and Rosie were puppies, Gloria and I introduced them to neighborhood children and to our young granddaughters. Also, on daily walks, when we encountered a child who asked, "Can I pet your doggies?" I'd pick up Molly and Rosie and let the child pet them.

Now when we walk, both Molly and Rosie tug at their leashes when they see kids in the distance. They want to get to them quickly. Relishing a tummy rub, Rosie usually rolls onto her back when a little kid greets her.

I'm glad my dogs are kid safe. Growing up today is hazardous enough without having to ward off aggressive dogs.

GOOD DOGMA

I don't know how much exposure Jesus' disciples had to children, but on one occasion they treated a bunch of kids gruffly. Matthew 19:13 reports that "little children were brought to Jesus for him to

place his hands on them. But the disciples rebuked those who brought them."
Apparently, the disciples perceived kids as unworthy of Jesus' time and interest.
How wrong they were!

Jesus said, "Let the little children come to me, and do not hinder them, for the
kingdom of heaven belongs to such as these" (v. 14). Then he placed his hands
on them and blessed them (v. 15; Mark 10:16).

Kids pick up quickly on how we perceive them. They know whether we value
them or see them simply as annoyances, ankle biters, or rug rats. Let's pray and
live in such a way that children will see Jesus' love and gentleness in the way we
relate to them.

A BIBLE TREAT

Whoever welcomes one of these little children in my name welcomes me.

(Mark 9:37)

41. *Feel Trapped?*

SPRINKLER SYSTEMS ARE an absolute necessity in Colorado's semiarid climate. Rain is too scarce and humidity is too low for grass to survive without the aid of a sprinkler system. But a sprinkler system can pose a challenge to people and dogs. I have pondered my fate more than once on a golf course upon seeing my ball roll under a sprinkler. Both club selection and timing must be perfect or else.

Molly sauntered into the backyard in response to nature's call one evening only to become trapped by our sprinkler system. The sprinklers in the zone nearest the back of the house had come on, leaving her no dry return route. Every time she tried to approach the house, a surge of water splattered her. Finally, she resigned herself to the fate of having to stay at the back of the yard until the sprinklers ran their course.

But I wouldn't let her suffer silently in the chill of failed escape attempts. I rushed through the spray, scooped her up in my arms, and rushed into the house. Despite getting wet, I felt like a hero. I had rescued Molly!

GOOD DOGMA

The Hebrews had left Egypt where they had been slaves, but Pharaoh's cavalry was in hot pursuit. With the cavalry behind them and the Red Sea in front of them, they felt trapped. They didn't know how to fight battles; they only knew how to make bricks. They were helpless, and their situation was hopeless. But God made a way of escape. He carved a path through the Red Sea and brought them safely across to the other side.

When the cavalry followed, God turned "the sprinkler system" back on. The water returned to its place and drowned the pursuers.

If you feel trapped in a situation you can't possibly handle alone, perhaps an unbearable job situation, over-the-eyebrows debt, or a crushing temptation, do what the Hebrews did. Stand firm and see the deliverance of the Lord (Exod. 14:13).

A BIBLE TREAT

No temptation has seized you except what is common to man. And God is faithful; he will not let you be tempted beyond what you can bear. But when you are tempted, he will also provide a way out so that you can stand up under it.

(1 Cor. 10:13)

42. *Hairless, but Not Friendless*

BECAUSE SHE IS A MALTESE, Molly has a full coat of soft, silky hair. If we let it grow out, it would reach the floor. Rosie, our toy poodle, also has a full coat of hair. Hers is red and curly. Since they are both females, I'm guessing they like their full-bodied and attractive coats. However, not long ago they befriended an almost hairless dog, proving they are neither puffed up with self-pride nor full of prejudice.

Our daughter, Sherrie, opened her heart and home to a rescued two-year-old Chinese crested. Guido has no hair except around his feet, at the end of his tail and on his head. Therefore he is not like most dogs, but he stole Sherrie's heart and proved to Gloria and me that he is an exceptionally good dog.

We did not know how our dogs would respond to Guido. Would they accept him, hairless as he is? Much to our delight, the three dogs got along well as soon as they met. The lack of hair wasn't ever an issue.

GOOD DOGMA

Christians who harbor prejudice in their hearts may be few, but they are still too many. Our fellowship should not exclude any believer or group of believers. Our arms should be open to embrace our brothers and sisters in Christ, regardless of their accent, skin color, age, level of education, social status, or physical attributes. We are family—the family of God. Each of us is simply a sinner saved by grace. If it were not for Christ's love and redeeming grace, we would be lost forever.

Jesus, a Jew, met a Samaritan woman at Jacob's well one day. Jews despised Samaritans, and this Samaritan was immoral; yet Jesus spoke to her politely. She was amazed at his kindness and as she listened to his words, she became aware that he was the Messiah—her Savior.

Before long, she brought a stream of Samaritans to the well to meet Jesus (John 4:1–39).

If we choose to honor Jesus, we will rid our lives of prejudice and reach out to everyone with his love.

A Bible Treat

There is neither Jew nor Greek, slave nor free, male nor female, for you are all one in Christ Jesus.

(Gal. 3:28)

43. Chasing Rabbits

A TWO-MILE PEDESTRIAN PATH winds its way through our neighborhood, through a park, and then between some nicely landscaped houses. At least once a day, I walk Molly and Rosie along this path. Most often our walk occurs just before sunset.

Rabbits seem to like the evening hours, too. I often see them hopping around shrubs, across lawns, and even in the pedestrian path. Even when I don't see a rabbit, I know it isn't far away. Molly and Rosie inform me of its proximity by yanking on their leashes suddenly and picking up the pace like horses heading home to their stable for fresh hay.

If I have Molly and Rosie on extended leashes, they stretch them to the limit in their frantic attempt to catch a rabbit. Little do they know that rabbits run faster than little dogs and are able to hide in thick brush. Furthermore, they never seem to get the message that chasing rabbits is a waste of time and energy.

GOOD DOGMA

Frankly, in my pastoral ministry, I have met Christians who chase rabbits. Instead of studying the Bible to learn about God and his will for them, they ignore the big picture depicted in a passage of Scripture and pursue rabbit trails instead.

They want to know what each toenail of Nebuchadnezzar's image represents. They ask why Antichrist is so, well, anti-Christ. Their rabbit chasing continues. If nothing is impossible with God, can he create a rock so heavy he can't lift it?

How can God be one, yet exist in three persons? Why did Jesus choose Judas as a disciple, knowing Judas would betray him?

The apostle Paul advised Titus, a pastor at Crete, to "avoid foolish controversies and genealogies and arguments and quarrels about the law, because these are unprofitable and useless" (Titus 3:9).

Doesn't it make sense to devote our time and energy to teaching that keeps our Christian walk focused and enjoyable? Let's keep a tight leash on all who try to pull us into their habit of chasing rabbits.

A BIBLE TREAT

Your word is a lamp to my feet and a light for my path.

(Ps. 119:105)

44. Fertilizer Food

"SIR, OUR LAWN FERTILIZER is totally organic. It contains nothing harmful to dogs."

"Okay," I replied, "fertilize both lawns."

After the application, I kept Molly and Rosie off both lawns for several hours in spite of the lawn care specialist's assurance that his product was harmless. In retrospect, I should have kept them off the lawns until the following day. Molly's visit to the backyard had no ill effects, but Rosie's did. She ingested some of the "harmless" fertilizer pellets and gave Gloria and me a night to remember.

Her violent shaking and vomiting began near midnight, and when it became clear that she was suffering severe stomach pain, we rushed her to an all-night emergency animal clinic. The diagnosis was a highly irritated stomach with some burning caused by ingesting fertilizer.

After the clinic staff administered a couple of injections, attached a water pouch under Rosie's skin and billed us $165, we took Rosie home. She slept soundly the rest of the night, and the next day regained her energy.

Next time a lawn care specialist tells me his fertilizer is harmless to dogs, I may ask him to eat some before he applies it.

GOOD DOGMA

Like "harmless" fertilizer, some religious teaching is injurious to spiritual health. First-century Christians had to cope with several religious teachings that contradicted healthful doctrine and, consequently, threatened to poison the churches. Legalism was one of those dangerous teachings. Its proponents argued

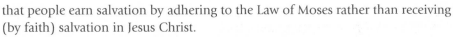

that people earn salvation by adhering to the Law of Moses rather than receiving (by faith) salvation in Jesus Christ.

The apostles warned the Galatian churches to beware of those who preach this false gospel (Gal. 1:6–9). Another poisonous teaching claimed Jesus was not truly human. They charged he also was not God incarnate.

Both Paul and John countered this evil teaching (2 Tim. 3:16 and 1 John 4:1–3). Others claimed Jesus was just a man, but Paul pointed out that Jesus is the very "image of the invisible God" and the creator of all things (Col. 1:15, 16).

Another poisonous teaching insisted that believers are free to sin. Paul exploded this myth in Romans 6 by assuring his readers that believers must not yield themselves to sin, but to God.

If even a kindly looking, soft-spoken, silver-haired, cherub-cheeked religious minister assures us his teaching is harmless, we ought to subject it to the light of Scripture. If it fails the test, we shouldn't apply it to our lives. Ingesting poisonous religion could cost us plenty.

A BIBLE TREAT

[An elder] must hold firmly to the trustworthy message as it has been taught, so that he can encourage others by sound doctrine and refute those who oppose it.
(Titus 1:9)

45. Thunder, Lightning, and a Safe Lap

COLORADO SPRINGS IS a very nice place to live, as are many other places in the United States and other free countries. The weather is especially pleasant here. We enjoy more than three hundred days of sunshine annually, and at an altitude of 6,300 feet above sea level, the sunshine tends to be brilliant. Clear and dazzling against a backdrop of cloudless blue skies, Pike's Peak, just west of the city, tops 14,000 feet and captures the "Oohs" and "Aahs" of both residents and tourists. Because humidity is very low, rain often evaporates without reaching the ground.

Having sounded like a well-paid employee of the Colorado Springs Chamber of Commerce, let me tell you about a downside to our weather. Big, billowing clouds may roll over the Rocky Mountains on a summer evening and bring sudden storms. Thunder resembles cannon blasts, lightning flashes like a zillion exploding firecrackers, and golf ball–size hail pummels everything around.

Mollie and Rosie show their fear of hostile weather. When lightning streaks across the sky and thunder erupts, they jump to what they must think is a safe place—my lap. It gets a little crowded in my recliner, but I don't mind a bit. They are welcome to stay there even after the storm has passed.

GOOD DOGMA

Have you read Psalm 23 recently? You may want to read it again and observe when the references to the Lord change from third person to second person. As the psalmist reflects on his relationship with the Lord—his shepherd—he refers to the Lord as "he" when everything is calm and pleasant.

"He makes me to lie down in green pastures, he leads me beside quiet waters, he restores my soul. He guides me in paths of righteousness" (vv. 2, 3).

But when life turns stormy for the psalmist, he switches to the more intimate second person pronoun "you." He writes, "Even though I walk through the valley of the shadow of death, I will fear no evil. For you are with me; your rod and your staff, they comfort me" (v. 4).

If life was all sunshine, and thunder and lightning never crashed and flashed around us, how well would we know the Lord's presence and feel his peace? Surely, the safest place to be in life's storms is in the presence of our Shepherd.

A Bible Treat

He who dwells in the shelter of the Most High will rest in the shadow of the Almighty. I will say of the LORD, "He is my refuge and my fortress, my God, in whom I trust."

(Ps. 91:1, 2)

46. Après Vous!

APRÈS VOUS! Isn't that how a toy poodle would say, "After you!" if it could talk? Rosie, our toy poodle, seems to think she has to wait for Molly to eat before she eats. My wife or I can place two dishes of food on the floor, one in front of Molly and the other in front of Rosie, but Rosie will not touch her food until Molly finishes hers.

I carry treats with me when I take Molly and Rosie for daily walks. As soon as we return home, both dogs sit and look up at me as if to say, "Okay, it's time to reward us for walking with you." If I offer Rosie a treat before offering one to Molly, she rejects it until Molly gets her treat.

Dogs must communicate with each other about such matters, and Molly has definitely told Rosie, "I'm the alpha dog and you are the omega."

GOOD DOGMA

Après vous (after you) is a French expression, but these two little words ought to translate into appropriate actions on the part of Christians around the world. A rule of life for many non-Christians seems to be, "Put yourself first," but Christians ought to march to the beat of a different drummer.

When two of Jesus' disciples requested seats next to him in the kingdom, he explained how things work in the kingdom of God. "Whoever wants to be great among you must be your servant," he said (Mark 10:43). He continued, "And whoever wants to be first must be slave of all" (v. 44).

Jesus illustrated what it means to put others first. In the Upper Room, he performed the duty of a slave by washing his disciples' feet (John 13). On the cross, he gave his life for others. Jesus practiced what he preached!

The world teaches us to look out for our own interests. It urges a mother to put her own interest ahead of her husband's and children's interests. It preaches do-whatever-it-takes-to-get-whatever-you-want messages to a dad. It persuades a CEO that he has a right to a gigantic bonus while the corporation sinks in a sea of red ink. It tells an employee it's okay to cheat on a test or pad an expense account for personal profit. And it assures a student the end justifies the means, making it okay to cheat on tests and skew financial records in order to beat others out of scholarship money and acceptance at the best colleges.

It may not be easy to put others first, but it's the right way. Indeed, it's the way Jesus traveled!

A BIBLE TREAT

For even the Son of Man did not come to be served, but to serve, and to give his life as a ransom for many.

(Mark 10:45)

47. Barking at the Wrong Crowd

I LIKE TO WATCH TV's "Animal Planet" channel, especially when it features dogs. The Westminster Kennel Club Dog Show and the Eukanuba All-Breed Championship Dog Show also rank high among my favorites. But a problem arises when I view these shows or watch a "Pet Adoption" segment of our local news.

Here's the problem. Molly and Rosie go wild when they see dogs on TV and even wilder when those dogs bark. They charge across the room, leap at the TV, and bark for all they're worth. When I switch channels, apparently they think the dogs leave the family room and go to the backyard. With as much sound and fury as little dogs can muster, they rush to the backyard in search of the canine intruders. What they fail to realize, of course, is the dogs on TV are simply images.

Barking at mere images is like barking at the wrong crowd. If aggressive dogs invaded our home or yard, I would likely tell Molly and Rosie, "Bark at that crowd."

GOOD DOGMA

Have you known Christians who bark at the wrong crowd? Often, they show up at church business meetings and make themselves obnoxious by complaining about a new expenditure or policy. They criticize the board's leadership or the length of the pastor's vacation. Any proposed revision to the church constitution drives them wild.

They crank up their barking to unbearable sound decibels. These are the same people who use the telephone to bark about the visitors who had the audacity to sit in their seats last Sunday. The kids who wiggle in church or the teens who talk and giggle are also targets for barking.

Like Molly's and Rosie's attacks on dogs appearing on TV, complaining, critical Christians usually bark at the wrong crowd. But they face a real foe they need to target. That foe is the devil. Instead of burning energy and venting grievances against fellow believers, every Christian should pray for them and encourage them to team up their forces against evil.

Paul decried the senseless barking among the Christians of the Galatian churches. He implored, "Love your neighbor as yourself" (Gal. 5:14). He also warned, "If you keep on biting and devouring each other, watch out or you will be destroyed by each other" (v. 15).

A BIBLE TREAT

Be imitators of God, therefore, as dearly loved children and live a life of love, just as Christ loved us and gave himself for us as a fragrant offering and sacrifice to God.

(Eph. 5:1, 2)

48. *Waiting to Be Rescued*

I'M GLAD MOLLY AND ROSIE have a safe home and owners who love them. But thousands of other dogs are homeless. Abandoned by owners or suffering the consequences of overbreeding, many homeless dogs live locked in cages or other confined spaces. Many suffer physical abuse. Some circle nervously hour upon hour because they are unable to run free. In all likelihood, they will never experience the fun of playing fetch or enjoy a friendly pat on the head.

Fortunately, some kind souls have dedicated themselves to rescuing homeless dogs and finding good homes for them. I suppose there are rescue groups for almost every breed, and certainly local animal shelters work hard to place all kinds of dogs.

In our community, almost every Saturday handlers wait with adoptable dogs at pet supply stores and hope a caring person or family will fall in love with a dog and adopt it. If I let my heart frame my decisions, I would adopt every dog that wagged its tail and cocked its head in my direction. But I know two dogs are enough for now, and I will do my best to make them feel loved.

If every good home would open its doors to a homeless dog, the world would be a much better place!

GOOD DOGMA

Christians should never be content to enjoy the safety and blessings of Jesus' fold. He said, "I have other sheep that are not of this sheep pen. I must bring them also" (John 10:16).

He is the Good Shepherd who left the ninety-nine sheep that were in the fold and searched for the one that was lost. When he found it, he lifted it onto his shoulders and brought it back to the fold.

As Jesus' followers, we should share his compassion for the lost and endeavor to rescue them. They can experience the love and security Jesus provides if we reach them in time.

A BIBLE TREAT

Suppose one of you has a hundred sheep and loses one of them. Does he not leave the ninety-nine . . . and go after the lost sheep until he finds it? And when he finds it, he joyfully puts it on his shoulders and goes home. Then he calls his friends and neighbors together and says, "Rejoice with me, I have found my lost sheep."

(Luke 15:4–6)

49. Rosie, the Imitator

IF IMITATION IS A SINCERE form of flattery, a whole lot of flattery is taking place. As soon as a reality show becomes successful, a raft of other reality shows spring up. A popular male movie sports a distinct hairstyle, and soon young men everywhere copy it. A female rock star drapes her pants low over her hips and wears a top that bares her navel, and before long a nation of teen girls follow her lead. Churches, too, imitate methods they believe are successful, patterning their worship, programs, and leadership styles after this or that megachurch.

Even Rosie, our toy poodle, flatters Molly by imitating her. If Molly jumps up, Rosie jumps up. If Molly barks to go out, Rosie barks to go out. If Molly lies down and nibbles at a toy, Rosie lies down and nibbles at a toy. I fear she may become a carbon copy of a Maltese. But I see a couple of notable differences.

On walks, Rosie assumes the lead and Molly trails behind. Also, when we encounter other dogs, Rosie yaps sharply and tugs at the leash in a mad effort to engage "the enemy," whereas Molly remains silent and calm. Apparently, there's still hope that Rosie will always be Rosie.

GOOD DOGMA

You have surely noticed that Christians are distinct from one another. Manuel is quiet. Manfred is kind of mouthy. Greta is a groupie. Gladys is a loner. Alan and Belinda are quick to enter a discussion during the young married couples' Bible study, but only a crowbar would pry Steve's and Rhonda's mouths open. I guess it does take all kinds to make the world go 'round!

God certainly doesn't create cookie cutter human beings, but in spite of our distinct personalities and individual preferences, Christians should be imitators. Not necessarily imitators of one another, but imitators of God.

Writing to the Ephesians, Paul counseled, "Be imitators of God, therefore, as dearly loved children" (Eph. 5:1). Knowing that God is righteous, we ought to lead righteous lives. Because God is loving and kind, we ought to demonstrate love and kindness in all our relationships. Because he is full of compassion, we ought to be compassionate. Because he forgave us, we ought to forgive others.

What might our homes, churches, and places of employment be like if we became excellent imitators of God? Perhaps we would start a trend!

A Bible Treat

Whoever serves me must follow me; and where I am, my servant also will be. My Father will honor the one who serves me.

(John 12:26)

50. High Maintenance

A COUPLE I KNOW purchased a Maltese puppy when Gloria and I brought Molly home from the "little house on the prairie." Several months later that couple gave their Maltese to relatives. They explained, "She was such a high-maintenance dog, it was too hard to care for her."

We have found that Molly, our Maltese, is also a high-maintenance dog, but we would never give her away. Even during her puppy stage, when caring for her was especially challenging, we cared too much for her to entertain a single thought of handing her to someone else. Sure, she has always required a lot of grooming because her long, silky hair becomes matted without combing and brushing, but doesn't everything of value require some high maintenance?

Owning a dog is almost like raising children. The family budget has to stretch to include food, toys, education (obedience training), and health care. Of course, one difference is dogs do not demand designer clothes. Like kids, dogs need attention and love. Also, they need baths and haircuts (even Guido, Sherrie's almost hairless Chinese crested, visits a groomer for a clipping and combing!).

No one should purchase a puppy without considering the cost of the pet's lifetime care. Only love for a firm commitment to man's best friend will translate "high maintenance" into "high privilege."

Good Dogma

It's nothing short of amazing that Jesus loved us enough to purchase us from the slave market of sin (1 Pet. 1:18, 19). But it is also amazing he cares so deeply for us that he accepts us as members of God's family.

After all, we are high-maintenance people. We need constant attention and love. Left to ourselves, we wander into trouble because temptation entices us away from the straight and narrow path. Trials and trouble cause us to ask the Lord to bail us out. Our lives often become matted and require untangling.

We do not always follow the Lord obediently. Our obedience training continues until we enter heaven. Nevertheless, the Lord will never abandon us. He promised, "Never will I leave you; never will I forsake you" (Heb. 13:5).

A Bible Treat

Being confident of this, that he who began a good work in you will carry it to completion until the day of Christ Jesus.

(Phil. 1:6)

51. The Good-bye We All Dread

THE HARDEST THING about owning a dog is saying good-bye for the last time. I have gone through this heart-wrenching experience twice. Our first toy poodle, Fluffy, graced our home from 1963 to 1976. Sadly, we had to put her to sleep because of heart failure and kidney damage. Fifi, our second toy poodle lived from 1977 to 1990. She, too, suffered irreversible ailments that required euthanasia.

Both Fluffy and Fifi grew up with our children. Each, in turn, was a playful and devoted friend. Words cannot describe the anguish I felt when I took each dog from my tear-filled family and handed her over to a veterinarian for the last time. Only someone who has known the love and loyalty of a dog—a close friend—can understand the grief parting brings.

The grief was so intense that I was certain I would never get another dog. But now I have two.

Occasionally, I think about those inevitable farewells that await Molly and Rosie, but I try to push such thinking away. I prefer to focus on the joy these two little dogs infuse into Gloria's life and mine today.

GOOD DOGMA

I suppose most dogs live about twelve or thirteen years. Their life span seems brief compared with that of most human beings. We can anticipate celebrating our seventieth birthday or our eightieth. Some of us may live to ninety or beyond. A few of us may reach the extraordinary age of one hundred. Nevertheless, in the normal course of events, all of us will say a final good-bye to this life. Hebrews 9:27 assures us that "man is destined to die."

For the Christian, death is a defeated foe because Jesus conquered it. He arose from the grave and demonstrated that all who believe in him have eternal life (2 Tim.1:8–10). Death is not the end of life; it is a passage to a fuller and unending one in heaven. It is a change of address, a graduation, and a home going.

Separation from Christian loved ones is merely temporary. Before long, we will all enjoy a joyful family reunion. Best of all, death ushers the Christian into the Savior's presence for a face-to-face meeting. Christians never say good-bye for the last time!

A Bible Treat

Jesus said to her [Martha], "I am the resurrection and the life. He who believes in me will live, even though he dies; and whoever lives and believes in me will never die. Do you believe this?"

(John 11:25, 26)

52. Do Good Dogs Go to Heaven?

"DR. DYET, DO DOGS HAVE A SOUL?" The question came to me by phone from a retired woman with five toy poodles—she called them her "children."

"The Bible tells us animals have a soul," I explained, "but it does not say they have a spirit. Only human beings have a spirit. The human spirit sets us apart from animals and gives us the capacity to worship God."

Her sobbing told me my theological answer was more than she wanted or needed. "Jacques died this morning," she cried. "Will I see him in heaven?"

Her question is not uncommon. What parent hasn't fielded that question from a child after losing the family pet? Adults as well as children hope the answer is, "Yes, you will see your dog in heaven."

My theology doesn't include a section on "dogology," so I can't promise anyone, including myself, that our departed canine companions are in heaven. But my theology does lead me to believe that heaven is a wonderful place of joy and countless attractions. Everything there will outshine and outclass everything here.

The best life offers here will be even better in heaven, so I wouldn't be surprised to find our beloved pets there. After all, at the beginning of the world when God created a paradise for the first two human beings, he included a wide variety of animals. Perhaps the paradise we call heaven will also include an animal population.

We do know that one day, Jesus and the armies of heaven will descend from heaven, "riding on white horses" (Rev. 19:11–14). If there are horses in heaven, then we have hope our good and faithful canine friends will be there, too!

GOOD DOGMA

Probably the biggest lie the devil has spread throughout the centuries is good people go to heaven. They don't. We do not receive a passport to heaven by trying to keep the Ten Commandments and being all-around good citizens or active church members.

The Bible states unequivocally that God receives into heaven only those who have trusted in his Son as Savior. "He who has the Son has life; he who does not have the Son of God does not have life," the apostle John wrote in 1 John 5:12. Furthermore, the apostle Paul wrote in Ephesians 2:8, 9 that we are not saved by works, but by grace through faith in Jesus Christ.

Safe passage to heaven is not about anything we do; it is all about what Jesus has done. He died to obtain our salvation, and he arose to prove that God, the Father accepted that work on our behalf.

Take time right now to thank Jesus for dying for you and opening wide heaven's door to welcome you.

A BIBLE TREAT

For the wages of sin is death, but the gift of God is eternal life in Christ Jesus our Lord.

(Rom. 6:23)